Get Smart!

Get Smart!

A Woman's Guide to Equality on Campus

Montana Katz and Veronica Vieland

The Feminist Press
at The City University of New York
New York

Published 1988 by The Feminist Press at The City
University of New York, 311 East 94 Street, New York, NY 10128
Distributed by The Talman Company, Inc., 150 Fifth Avenue, New York,
NY 10011

Printed in the United States of America

91 90 89 88 5 4 3 2 1

Library of Congress Cataloging-in-Publication Data

Katz, Montana.
  Get smart!
  Bibliography: p.
  1. Women—Education (Higher)—United States.
2. Sex discrimination in education—United States.
3. Educational equalization—United States. I. Vieland, Veronica. II. Title.
LC1756.K36 1988   376'.65'0973   88-21450
ISBN 0-935312-86-2
ISBN 0-935312-87-0 (pbk.)

Text design by Paula Martinac

This publication is made possible, in part, by public funds from the New York
State Council on the Arts.

Course Guide

Orientation

Why is it that the term "coed" is only used to refer to women? After all, coed is a shortening of the word "coeducation," which refers to the education of women and men together. It seems, then, that the term coed should be used to refer to *any* student in a coeducational institution. But somehow, only women are called coeds. The use of the term coed suggests that women are special cases on college campuses; that it is the inclusion of women that makes a school coeducational, not the *mixture* of women and men. This usage suggests that college is principally a man's world. But this is a very peculiar way of looking at things.

At the present time, women make up approximately 53 percent of all undergraduate students and 48 percent of all graduate students in the country. Overall, women now represent 52.5 percent of all students in higher education in the United States. That's more than half![1]

What's more, students are not the only women on campus. When you go to register, who's sitting behind the registration desk? If you have a question about registration, whom do you talk to in the registrar's office? When you go to pay your bills, who hands you the receipt? In the cafeteria, who serves your food? Who cleans your dormitory? When you make an appointment to see a professor, who sits behind the secretary's desk? Who helps you with a reference problem in the library? Whom do you talk to about an appointment at the health service?

Sometimes the doctor you see at the health service is a woman. Some of your professors are women. If you ever have occasion to talk with a dean, the dean may also be a woman. From administrators to clerical workers, from health services staff to faculty, women are to be found in every corner of the university. It has been estimated that women constitute as much as 49 percent of the total number of university employees in the country. This means that on the average United States college or university campus, women account for about 51 percent of the total campus population. That's also more than half!

---

[1] *Digest of Education Statistics 1987* (Washington, DC: Center for Education Statistics, 1987), Tables 101, 104

Despite the overwhelming predominance of women on the campus, however, women students continue to face a variety of problems that can seriously affect their ability to get the most out of their education. For example, a recent study conducted at Harvard University corroborated the view that sexual harassment is a widespread problem on university campuses. The study revealed that 32 percent of the tenured female faculty, 49 percent of the untenured female faculty, 41 percent of the female graduate students, and 34 percent of the female college students have encountered sexual harassment from a person in authority on campus at least once while at the university.[2]

Women are more likely than men to be in need of financial aid while in college. Nevertheless, a 1981–82 study showed that women in college received 72 cents in grant money for every dollar received by men; earned 68 cents to every dollar earned by men; and, borrowed 84 cents to every dollar borrowed by men. On the whole, women have greater unmet financial need than men during their college years.[3]

Other studies have shown that women suffer a significant decline in academic and career aspirations over their college years; women students also tend to feel less confident about their preparation for graduate and professional school than do men attending the same colleges.[4]

Clearly, there is something wrong with the education women are receiving in college.

Get Smart is designed to help women get the best college education they can, unhampered by problems that would not affect them if they were men. It is intended for women students of all ages, races, and backgrounds: recent high school graduates and returning women students; minority students and white students; full-time students and part-time students; students at small rural colleges and students at large urban universities. Professors, administrators, and other educators will also find this book useful in helping them provide the best education to their women students.

Get Smart is a handbook—a how-to book. It was written to show women students how to see problems before they become serious and how to handle them on the spot. It shows you how to take control. In the course of reading this book, you will learn how you

[2] *On Campus with Women* 13, no. 3 (Winter 1984).
[3] *On Campus with Women* 13, no. 4 (Spring 1984).
[4] Joseph Katz and Rodney Hartnett, *Scholars in the Making* (Cambridge: Ballinger, 1975).

can recognize those aspects of the college experience that might otherwise work against you, and turn them to your educational advantage.

We recommend that you read the whole book through from cover to cover. Many of the ideas and issues discussed may apply to situations you have not yet encountered, but will at some point in the future. Thus, the book can be used as a general consciousness raising tool. Afterward, you may want to refer only to those sections of the book that pertain to particular problems you may be having.

Each of the first four chapters is divided into a "Problems" section and a "Solutions" section. In the "Problems" sections we discuss the difficulties that women may encounter on campus. In the "Solutions" sections we discuss the many solutions that the student has available to her.

Here's what each chapter covers:

Get Smart Course 101 looks at what goes on in the classroom. Interaction between professors and students during class can teach women to lower their expectations for themselves. This chapter examines how this works and what can be done about it.

Get Smart Course 202 considers one-on-one relationships between male professors and female students. These relationships are complex and often difficult. But they are also important to the college experience. The chapter talks about the dynamics of these relationships and how to best negotiate them.

Faculty make many decisions that affect the college educations of their students—from assigning grades for written work to hiring teaching and research assistants. Faculty decision making can be biased against women in subtle and largely unrecognized ways. **Get Smart Course 303** explains why, and presents some simple and effective ways to counteract potential difficulties.

Get Smart Course 404 looks at university policies that may be discriminatory in their impact on women. It is the responsibility of university administrations to correct these policies. But you need to know how to recognize them, and what to do if one of them is presenting you with an educational obstacle.

Get Smart Course 505 is about the law. Under the law you are entitled to an educational opportunity equal to that of your male peers. This chapter discusses what this means in practical terms, as

well as the possibilities and limitations of using the courts for redress. Even if you never have cause to contemplate a law suit, you
should know your rights and entitlements.

Finally, **Commencement** puts the student's experience into the
broader context of the university as a social system. It is a system
with some old and bad habits, and old habits die hard. But this book
provides a lesson in empowerment: at Commencement, you will see
how putting your power to work for you will help break those old
habits and bring in much better ones.

We wrote this book in order to help you secure your fair share of
the educational opportunities your college has to offer. We look forward to the day when a book like this is a curious relic of the past.
You have the power to help bring this about. This book will show
you how to develop that power.

We would like to thank the following people for advice that im-
proved the manuscript: Lisa Leizman, Alfred Nordmann, Janusz Or-
dover, and Constance Vieland. Above all in this respect our
appreciation goes to Florence Howe and Joanne O'Hare of The Feminist Press for helping us produce a better book. In addition, Bernice
Sandler provided encouragement and assistance well beyond our expectations. And finally, we would like to give special thanks to Joseph Katz whose enthusiasm, persistence, and counsel helped turn
the manuscript into this book.

Get Smart!

Get Smart
Course 101

The Classroom:
Making It Work for You

The classroom is the focus of every student's college experience. That's where you receive instruction in particular subject matter. But what goes largely unnoticed is that the classroom is also where you receive instruction in forming a perception of yourself as a student. This instruction is often subtle and tacit. As we look closely at some aspects of what goes on in the classroom, we will see that one and the same class can offer two completely different curricula: one for the women and one for the men. The fact that most of this **hidden curriculum** goes unnoticed does not mean that it is without effect. By the time you finish reading this chapter, you may see ways in which you've been getting more of an education than you bargained for!

As you read through this chapter, remember that the hidden curriculum is a course of study just like any other. It has principles that can be learned, but whether you choose to believe them or to apply them to your own life is entirely up to you. The "Solutions" section of the chapter will provide you with techniques for recognizing when the hidden curriculum is being taught in your classes, and for developing the power to choose which of its lessons you accept. At the same time, you will be learning to create a fruitful classroom environment for yourself and the students around you.

Problems

College is a place where many decisions concerning your future are made more or less definitely and more or less consciously. You make decisions about what courses to take and what field to major in. These decisions in turn affect, though not irrevocably, the sort of work you may choose after college and the choices you will make about continuing your education in graduate or professional school. You also make decisions about what courses not to take and what fields to avoid, as well as what careers not to consider and what future education not to pursue. Sometimes you make these decisions deliberately and consciously, but sometimes you just fail to consider certain options as real possibilities.

In addition, your choices are to some extent governed by hunches, biases, and accidents. For example, you might have a hunch that you won't like calculus, and so never enroll for a course in it. Or you might happen to have a particularly inspiring professor in a biology course, and choose to go on to more advanced biology courses. Or you might feel that the field of art history is too "soft," and so choose another major, although art history particularly interests you.

You may never know what your hunch about calculus is based on, or why that particular professor was so inspiring, or what it is exactly about art history that puts you off. You might never understand such feelings completely, but this chapter will alert you to some of the ways that your decision making may be affected by aspects of the college environment of which you are not presently aware. Once you become aware of them, you will have taken a large step toward making sure that you've really considered all your options, and that by ruling out possibilities you haven't sold yourself short.

Learning how to assess your real talents and interests is an important part of a good education. The hidden curriculum may be interfering with this crucial part of your education, but the hidden curriculum can be changed.

Student-Professor Interaction in Class

Let's look at some typical classroom situations and try to discern the hidden curriculum that students are being exposed to. We start by accompanying a hypothetical student—we'll call her "Anna"—as she goes to her class in Critical Thinking, a required course for all first-year students at her college.

One form of the hidden curriculum is taught through professor-student interaction in the classroom. Pay attention to the way the professor in this class interacts with Anna, and you will begin to see how this works.

Anna always goes to her Critical Thinking class well prepared, because she enjoys the lectures and the coursework. When she reads the assigned chapters in the textbook, she often comes up with a list of questions about the material, which she brings with her to the next class. The professor encourages classroom discussion and always invites questions from the students at the end of the class. In spite of this encouragement, Anna almost never leaves the classroom feeling satisfied. Though Anna keeps raising her hand, she seldom gets called on to ask her question. And when she is called on, she frequently has the feeling that her question is dealt with very quickly or is even brushed aside. Rarely does she have the feeling that the professor thinks the question a good one, or that it is worth answering in any detail. Twice she asked a question that was dealt with this way, but then later in the class another student—in both cases a man—asked what Anna thought was the same question as hers, and the professor treated it very seriously, as though it hadn't already been asked. Anna begins to notice that other women receive the same treatment, although fewer and fewer women talk in the class.

Anna happens to be fairly confident of her understanding of what she is studying, and she is quite sure that the questions she asks are intelligent and serious. Because she is relatively sure of herself, she is able to perceive the professor's treatment of her as in some way odd. Without such faith in her own intelligence, she might tend to assume that her questions are stupid or poorly articulated. She would probably not even notice that the professor treats her differently than the men in the class. Anna would simply get the message that what she has to say is trivial. She might very well soon stop asking questions in class; the pleasure she takes in the lectures might soon diminish; and even her enthusiasm for the subject might lessen as she becomes increasingly convinced of her incompetence in this class. Even given Anna's confidence, it isn't long before asking questions becomes almost a chore for her. And although she persists, she finds herself hesitating before each question, anticipating that it will not be well received.

Anna's Critical Thinking class presents a good example of how

women and men in a class are taught different lessons about themselves as students. From the point of view of its subject matter, this
class has all the makings of a productive educational environment.
The professor is probably at least in part responsible for inspiring
Anna's enthusiasm for the subject, and, by encouraging questions
and discussion in class, the professor gives the students a cue that
they should share and pursue their doubts, confusions, and interests
in the classroom. But the professor is treating the women and the
men in the class differently, and in so doing is teaching the lesson
that the women are not to be taken as seriously as students as the
men. Every time the professor fails to give due consideration to a
question asked by a woman, or ignores her altogether, while consistently giving more attention to the men when they raise their hands
to ask questions, the professor is reinforcing a pattern of socialization
that teaches both women and men to think of women as lesser students.

Anna is even more acutely aware of this problem in her Principles
of Management course. She attends this class with her roommate,
Betty, two days a week at 1:10. Anna and Betty meet for lunch on
those days and then go to class together. They notice that as the
semester progresses, they have a harder time leaving the cafeteria in
time for class. They arrive later and later, and sometimes they don't
get there at all. They decide to talk about why this is happening
before their grades start to suffer.

Anna and Betty decide that the problem has nothing to
do with the subject matter itself, which they both find
interesting. The problem seems to stem from what takes
place during class. The class is divided into groups of four
or five students, and most of the class time is spent working out assigned management problems in these small
groups. At the end of each class, the groups come together
and present their solutions. Anna and Betty are in the only
group that consists solely of women, and although there
are women in the other groups, women seldom make the
group presentations at the end of class. As Anna and Betty
talk, they become aware of the difference between the
comments the professor makes when their group presents, compared to other groups. Their solutions have been
referred to as "naive" and "intuitive but unworkable,"
while the professor is fairly consistent in offering encouragement along with criticism to the other groups, saying,
for instance, "That's a very good start, though here's a
way in which you could extend your solution to make it

more workable. . . .'' Anna thinks this discrepancy is particularly pronounced when she speaks for her group. She timidly asks Betty, "Don't you think when I present it only makes things worse?"

Betty immediately and quite correctly points out that things may be worse when Anna presents, but it is not because Anna isn't a good presenter. The problem, they decide, has more to do with the fact that Anna is black, and, in fact, is the only black student in the class. While individual white women may not be singled out for criticism as long as they participate as working members of groups in which men generally present, an all-female working group has a tough time. An all-female group represented by a black student may have an even tougher time. Anna is made to bear the brunt of this situation.

Business management is an area generally understood to be "male": men tend to dominate the field, and most people have a harder time envisioning a woman in a true leadership position in business than a man. What may be even harder still for most people is to envision a black person in a position of power in a hierarchy in which many white people participate.

Professors' preconceptions about the appropriateness of certain fields for specialization by women, or their biases about the general capacity of women to excel in certain fields, may exacerbate the problem of differential treatment in the classroom. The hidden curriculum, while it can certainly be taught in any area, may be more pronounced in fields commonly thought of as men's fields: mathematics, engineering, political science, and others. It may also be more acutely experienced by individual women in these fields, since, unless they attend women's colleges, they are likely to constitute a minority in the classroom. The situation can be further complicated by biases such as the racist one faced by Anna.

The professor need not deliberately discourage the women in the class, and is probably not even aware of the differential treatment accorded to the women and men in class or of singling Anna out for discouraging treatment. But intentional or otherwise, the professor's behavior is not producing good effects on Anna or Betty. Moreover, especially because professors may not be aware of the existence of the hidden curriculum at all, the ways in which their communication with male and female students differs can be quite subtle.

For example, the professor may use an impatient or patronizing tone of voice with the women in the class, compared to a more serious and interested tone reserved for the men. Accompanying the professor's intonation may be nonverbal gestures that also signify the degree of the professor's interest or the professor's assessment of what is being said. The professor may nod or look attentive and pensive when listening to the men in the class, making frequent eye contact and giving serious responses. In contrast, the professor may glance at the clock or rearrange papers in a briefcase while listening to the women, make dismissive gestures such as shoulder shrugging, avoid eye contact, and generally make brief and offhand responses. A professor may stand tall and serious, perhaps in front of the blackboard, in responding to men, and may sit on the edge of the desk in a casual pose in responding to women.

Women's Questions/Men's Questions

Another way the hidden curriculum can be taught is through the kinds of questions directed to women and to men during class. Let's look at a couple of examples.

Consuela is taking a course in the history of Italian painting. At one lecture, the professor is showing slides of Giotto's Sistine Chapel. It just so happens that Consuela recently wrote a paper on this subject, and has a great many ideas about the work. At one point during the lecture, the professor asks if someone could describe the mood of the painting being shown, and calls on Consuela for an answer. When Consuela is finished, the professor asks the class in what way the formal elements of the painting contribute to the mood. For an answer to this question, the professor calls on one of the men in the class. Consuela wishes that the second question had been directed to her, since it would have given her much more of a chance to show how much she had already thought about the painting.

In this case, the professor asked Consuela to answer a question calling for a "subjective" response, one in which she had to explain how the painting made her feel or what it suggested to her. When the professor wanted an answer to the more abstract question about the relation of the form of the painting to the subjective experience, a man was called on. This was immediately frustrating to Consuela, who was prepared to give what she felt was an interesting answer to the second question. One incident of this sort may be trivial, but

Consuela may have this experience repeatedly and in many different classes, until it becomes a real problem for her.

Diane has a related problem.

Diane is rather shy and doesn't particularly enjoy speaking in class. One day in her education course, the professor calls on Diane to answer a question. The question is: At what age do children normally begin to learn their first language? This is a simple, factual question, and Diane is relieved that in order to answer it she doesn't have to say very much. Later in the class, the professor calls on a man, and asks him to explain the difference between two theories of language acquisition. Diane notes nervously how much more involved that question is than the one she had to answer, and is glad hers was so simple. As the term proceeds, Diane becomes more and more relaxed in this course, because she finds that when she is called on, she's never expected to answer difficult or abstract questions or to express her views at any length.

Although Consuela and Diane have different attitudes toward being called on to answer questions, they are both being exposed to the same hidden curriculum. Men are frequently expected to respond to the more abstract or complex questions or problems, while women may be called on to answer more concrete, factual questions. This pattern of expectations deprives women of opportunities to demonstrate their competence to deal with complex and abstract matters. But there's another problem, too.

The cumulative effect of being asked only certain limited questions while other students are asked complex questions is to lessen one's sense of competence to deal with complex matters. This is just as true whether the individual student feels frustrated or comforted by the practice. What feels comfortable to Diane may not necessarily be better for her. Furthermore, when a specific group of people is dealt with fairly regularly in this way, it reinforces the idea that the members of the group are systematically different from the rest—in this case, that women are less capable students than men.

It is highly likely that in most classrooms where differential treatment of women and men goes on, neither the professor nor the students are aware of the systematic difference between questions directed to women and questions directed to men. Nevertheless, such patterns of differential treatment give cues to students about what the professor expects of the different students and, therefore, about what the students can expect of themselves and of one another.

You might have noticed that the gender of the professors in these examples has not been specified. It is just as possible for female professors to engage in communicating this hidden curriculum in classroom interaction with students as it is for male professors. The tendency to perpetuate the hidden curriculum does not generally come from malice on the part of the professor, but from expectations of students, formed in turn by the socialization of the professors themselves. Since both female and male *students* are exposed to the same hidden curriculum concerning the competence of women as students, female as well as male *teachers* tend to hold different, and systematically lower, expectations for the women in their classes than for the men.

These lower expectations show up in many of the same ways regardless of whether the professor is female or male. However, the particular way in which a professor communicates these lower expectations will vary from professor to professor. Some professors may respond in an overly enthusiastic manner to answers given by women. A student receiving what seems like excessive praise for having answered a simple question is getting the message that the professor does not expect a great deal of her. A student who receives a high grade on a paper she knows is poor, especially if it is awarded by a professor known to grade harshly, may be just as disconcerted as a student who receives a low grade on a paper she knows is good.

There is no simple rule for determining when the hidden curriculum is being taught. It is characterized by the systematic differential treatment of women and men. Regardless of the behavior that is used to communicate the hidden curriculum, it forms a pattern of treatment of women that differs from treatment of men in the classroom.

We've been talking about the effect of the hidden curriculum on women in the classroom. Let's turn for a moment to its effect on men. Many aspects of the hidden curriculum that constitute problems for the women in the class serve to enhance the self-confidence of the men and to lower the men's opinions of the women as peers in the classroom.

For instance, consider what happens when a professor tends to be more attentive to men's comments and questions in class than to those of women. Most students, male or female, will not notice a systematic difference, and therefore the interaction between the professor and a particular student will be interpreted as a reflection of the professor's assessment of that particular student. Thus, just as a woman receiving flippant treatment in response to a question may tend to assume that her question is stupid or that her articulation of it is poor, a man receiving praise and thoughtful response from a professor will be likely to assume that this attention is an indication of the professor's favorable assessment of his abilities and perhaps his intelligence in general. The counterpart to the negative lesson that the hidden curriculum teaches women is a positive lesson it teaches men. The men are constantly encouraged and reinforced in their sense of themselves as competent students.

At the same time, the hidden curriculum tends to teach the men in the class to have a low opinion of the abilities of their female peers. The same situations that provide the men with a positive self-image serve to instill the belief that the women in the class are not as capable, interesting, or intelligent as the men. If the professor, as a rule, indicates a lower expectation for any particular woman in the class than for the men, then the perception of the men that as a rule the women are inferior students is reinforced.

And it goes without saying that the hidden curriculum teaches women lessons about other women in their classes as well.

Emma has just returned to college after having left in her sophomore year, thirty years earlier. If women have a tendency to feel out of place in some fields or class-rooms, older women feel doubly out of place. Emma feels conspicuous and self-conscious sitting in a roomful of eighteen- and nineteen-year-olds in her calculus course. But she resolves early on not to let this detract from the education she has come back for, and she makes a point of asking questions in class. The professor's response is often patronizing or belittling.

Emma persists in asking questions, and chooses to ignore the professor's tone of voice in the interest of getting what she needs out of the course. But the other women in the class may uncritically and unwittingly accept the lesson that older women warrant not respect but condescension.

Student Behavior

The effectiveness of the hidden curriculum can be seen in the students' behavior in the classroom. Pay attention to the ways in which women and men phrase their questions when they speak in class. Men tend to have a direct and assertive style, generally expressing self-confidence in their way of speaking. But women tend to speak in a hesitant, deferential style, frequently prefacing questions with apologies or disclaimers, as does our next hypothetical student, Fay. This is something you can observe in yourself and others.

Fay speaks up fairly regularly in some of her classes. She's aware that she almost always prefaces her classroom remarks with something like, "I'm sorry, maybe this point has already been covered, but . . . ," or, "I'm probably just missing the point, but. . . ." Sometimes she notices that she gives a question intonation to a sentence that she intends as a statement; for example, "I believe that point was covered in the text?" Even though she's aware of this habit, Fay has a hard time changing it, since in each instance the apology or disclaimer seems appropriate to her. She notices that she's not the only woman in her classes who does this sort of thing, although she has yet to hear a man apologize in class for what he's about to say.

Fay's constant apologies and disclaimers are a response to certain features of her environment and socialization. Her feeling that these qualifications are appropriate may reflect the "appropriateness" of a woman's expressing humility and deference in a classroom setting more than the appropriateness of an apology relative to the particular comment she then makes. The long-term effects of the practice, on both Fay herself and others in her classes, can be to reinforce the perception that she is less competent than someone who speaks assertively, regardless of the content of her remarks.

Professors' expectations and students' ways of presenting themselves can combine in other ways as well to support the view that women make less competent students than men. Women may tend to speak less often in class than men, to speak more quietly than the men, and to be much quicker to drop their questions altogether at the first sign of impatience on the part of the professor. Male students may routinely interrupt women, and professors may do nothing to remedy situations in which women are cut off in mid-sentence by their male peers. Women, on the other hand, rarely cut off a man while he is speaking in class. This asymmetry can produce a situation in which, even when women are trying to speak in class, the floor is dominated by the men. A man's comment may routinely be remarked upon and credited both by other students and by the professor, as when someone says, "That was an interesting point John made, and I'd like to get back to it." On the other hand, there may be little or no follow-up on a woman's remarks, and even when there is, she will rarely be credited by name.

All of this reflects the existence of the hidden curriculum. All of it indicates the extent to which its lessons have been learned. All of it can be changed.

Classroom Language

Another way in which the hidden curriculum is taught in the classroom is by means of language, for example, the general use of so-called generic masculine terms. An anthropology professor describing how to classify artifacts may say, "First the anthropologist must lay out all of his artifacts in groups which he has classified by. . . ." A philosophy professor may say, "Today in class we are going to discuss human nature. Let's start by seeing what distinguishes man from the other animals." Students may follow this practice as well, using the pronouns *he* and *him* for references to people except when explicit reference to a woman is intended.

It is not hard to see the effect of this practice in the hidden curriculum. If a name is used, the anthropology professor will almost certainly dub the hypothetical anthropologist who is classifying artifacts as "Mr." and not "Ms." Think of how peculiar this sentence sounds: "First the anthropologist—let's call him Ms. Jones—must lay out all of his artifacts." The fact is, as soon as the masculine pronoun is used generically in this way, the natural tendency is to assume that the character who is being referred to is indeed male.

The practice of using generic masculine terms is changing on many campuses, but it is still widespread. And in the classroom, it takes a particular toll. The student who hears, for instance, anthropologists consistently referred to using masculine terms develops an image of the "essential" anthropologist as male. If the student is a woman, this makes it difficult for her to picture herself as an anthropologist. Since this practice goes on in virtually all fields, female students face an obstacle in forming perceptions of themselves as potential professionals that their male peers do not. Indeed, their male peers have a headstart in forming such perceptions of themselves, since the pattern of speech reinforces their conception of professionals as men. When we combine this with the fact that most professors are men, and most of the people studied in college are men, then we see a crucial aspect of the hidden curriculum at work. The hidden curriculum makes it difficult for women to see themselves as belonging to the professional or academic world.

The use of generics is frequently combined with the use of stereotypes. If people in general are referred to using masculine terms, feminine terms may be reserved for people in certain professions, such as nursing or elementary school teaching. In addition, masculine terms may be used to refer to any hypothetical character in a position of power, strength, or mastery, or someone who exhibits such traits as fortitude or bravery. Feminine terms, on the other hand, may be used when speaking of hypothetical characters in passive, weaker, less competent, or less virtuous roles. For instance, a typical medical anecdote may involve a doctor who is referred to with male pronouns and a patient who is consistently referred to with female pronouns. Such practices contribute to the hidden curriculum by reinforcing peoples' prejudices concerning what women are "suited for" or capable of.

When enough people engage in this sort of stereotyping over a long period of time, it comes to seem that certain occupations or roles are more natural to one sex or the other. Not only do you not see many female car mechanics, for instance, but it even *sounds* funny to say, "The mechanic at that garage must really know her business!"

While this practice of stereotyping is changing, it is important to bear in mind that it can affect your judgment of what work or activities are appropriate to you as a woman. The fact that almost all professionals whom you hear discussed in the classroom—both hypothetical and real—will be men, or will be referred to by masculine terms, can make it more difficult for you to envision yourself as a potential member of the profession. Thus the hidden curriculum makes it difficult for women to view themselves not only as full and equal members of the academic community but as participants in a large number of activities they might choose to pursue after leaving the university.

Male Professors Teaching the Hidden Curriculum
So far it has been immaterial whether the professor we are discussing is male or female. But certain lessons of the hidden curriculum are taught primarily by men, and not by women. In the next example, generic usage and stereotyping shade off into something less subtle. This example takes place in a political science seminar on the concept of equal opportunity. The professor in this case is male.

> The professor had been talking about what goes on in hiring decisions when an employer must choose between rival job candidates "whom he judges to be equally well qualified for the work." The professor uses the example of an executive, referred to as "Mr. Smith," who wants to hire a secretary. Mr. Smith is considering two candidates, whom the professor calls "Betty" and "Boop," who have

> equivalent secretarial skills. The professor states that since the candidates are equally qualified for the job, Mr. Smith must choose on the basis of non–job-related attributes. Thus, the professor explains, Mr. Smith might legitimately choose to hire the "more shapely" candidate.

This single example, when used in a classroom, teaches several aspects of the hidden curriculum at once. The generic use of *he* at the outset is a problem. And the story employs the stereotypes of a male executive in a position of authority and power and female secretaries in dependent positions.

Notice the way the difference in status of the characters in the story is signaled by the forms of address chosen. The male employer is referred to by the formal title "Mr.", while the female secretaries are referred to by first name alone, and comic-strip first names at that. The choice of forms of address signals not only that the executive is considered male and the secretaries female but that executives, or, perhaps, male executives, are deserving of greater deference or respect than secretaries.

Pay attention to the way in which forms of address are used in day-to-day speech. Are all professors referred to as "Professor So-and-so"? Are some referred to by last name alone in some contexts? Are female professors ever referred to by last name alone? Are you more comfortable calling a female professor by her first name than a male professor? What about the secretarial staff: Are secretaries addressed by first or last name? Forms of address are used to reinforce hierarchical social structures. The names chosen in the anecdote reinforce the lower status of the two women relative to the man.

One aspect of the professor's example raises a different kind of issue. The professor wants to give an example of an attribute that is non–job-related. Since the job applicants are women, it might appear that being "shapely" is an obvious attribute. But this reference to a woman's appearance is entirely gratuitous and irrelevant to any substantive issues concerning equal opportunity, the subject matter of the seminar. If the introduction of this consideration doesn't strike you as peculiar, try replacing the two women in the example with two blacks, or two Jews. Imagine if the professor had said the employer could legitimately choose the applicant with lighter skin or a smaller nose!

The gratuitous reference to a woman's shape serves a function in communicating the hidden curriculum. It separates women from men: the women are the ones whose "shapeliness" counts. If the peculiarity goes unnoticed by the students, it is because they have already absorbed a good deal of the hidden curriculum. In this case, the view of the women in the class that they are systematically different from the men in the class is reinforced by virtue of the importance of their figures. If the peculiarity is noticed by women in the class, then it serves to reinforce their sense of being singled out by physical attributes at a time when they should be considered *students,* not females.

Classroom Fraternity and Women

The reference to female anatomy has one other very important effect: it creates a sort of bond, or fraternity, between the professor and the male students, to the exclusion of the female students. The male students can in some sense identify with the employer in the story, and can to some extent identify with the consideration of the applicants' shapeliness as a possible criterion. The female students are not likely to have an easy time identifying with an employer who takes into account the shapeliness of the applicants, even if they can identify themselves with the male employer, since whether the applicants are male or female, it is difficult to imagine a female executive caring about the applicants' figures.

But beyond this, since it is the professor who makes up the story and introduces the consideration of anatomy as legitimate, *the male students can identify with the professor* as he tells the story. The female students cannot. In this way, a fraternity is formed between the male students and their male professor. Hence the anecdote chosen for pedagogic purposes serves to foster an exclusion of the women present in the class.

This exclusion can be achieved more explicitly as well. For instance, as a preface to an example or an anecdote, a male professor may begin with a phrase such as, "Suppose that you are married and that your wife . . ."; or, "When you were a little boy. . . ." Even if one if not always aware of the peculiarity of the phrase at the time it is used, the cumulative effect of taking such forms of expression for granted in the classroom over a period of years is to form a bond between the men as members of the "included" group and to perpetuate the perception of individual women that they are members of the "excluded" group.

The exclusion of women can also be accomplished with explicit jokes through which a male professor forms a fraternity with the men in the class, as in our next example, which occurs in a physics course that Gina is attending.

One day in Gina's physics course, the male professor
was demonstrating an experiment about electron activity
under certain conditions. After the experiment, he put a
diagram on the board which represented this activity. The
diagram had a shape reminiscent of an hourglass. In order
to introduce some levity into a rather uneventful experiment, the professor remarked with a chuckle, "Don't you
wish they were all shaped like this?!"

Here we have a reference to female anatomy that is much more
explicit in its message of exclusion than the one in the previous example. The professor may sincerely mean only to introduce a little
levity into the discussion, but the joke he chooses is by no means
innocent, and its various messages all serve to undermine the sense
of belonging that the women students in the class should have. There
is no question that the "you" the professor is addressing refers only
to the men, and that the "they" refers only to women. Clearly the
joke does not work if it is supposed to appeal to the women's desire
that all men be shaped like hourglasses. So the women are not addressed, but are referred to as "they" in a remark made to the men.
Even though they are in the room, the professor talks *as if they were
not*. The remark is not only insulting, it carries the message that from
the professor's point of view, the women in the class do not constitute significant presences in the room.

The Official Curriculum
The hidden curriculum offers women lessons in exclusion not only
through what is said and done in the classroom but through the texts
used in courses as well. Not only does the undergraduate at most
universities have very few female professors as role models, but the
content of the standard "official" curriculum is almost entirely de-
void of references to women who have contributed to the develop-
ment of Western culture, and there have been many, in virtually
every area of study.

How often have you heard of the ancient Greek philosopher Hy-
patia, the computer pioneer and inventor of compilers Grace Hopper, the Mexican painter Frieda Kahlo, or the seventeenth-century
playwright, poet, and novelist Aphra Behn, who wrote thirteen nov-
els some thirty years before Daniel Defoe wrote his first novel (although he is commonly credited with having written the first novel)!
And when you do encounter a woman in a classroom discussion,

how often is she dealt with solely as a wife or helper of a man, for instance, as when Simone de Beauvoir is referred to as "Sartre's mistress"? How often does a diminutive adjective get placed before her name, such as "the minor poet Sappho"? How often is her contribution understated by restricting the field of comparison, as in "Ntozake Shange, one of the great black women dramatists of our time"?

Forms of address can also be used to distinguish women from men as the subjects of classroom study or discussion. It is standard practice in the classroom to refer to a male scholar, scientist, or artist simply by his last name, or in formal contexts by the title "Professor" or "Doctor." Women scholars, on the other hand, are frequently referred to with the prefix "Miss" or "Mrs." In this case, the inclusion of the formal title before the name introduces a distinction between women and men.

The primary texts you read can teach the hidden curriculum as well. A standard liberal arts education will expose the student to a large number of primary texts, from Aristotle to Hobbes to Freud, that may explicitly express damaging and denigrating views of women which may go completely unchallenged in class. If these views are not critically addressed, students in effect learn that they are not offensive.

The textbooks used in your classes may present several simultaneous examples of these kinds of exclusion. In a particularly blatant example, the two passages quoted below are from a textbook on the computer programming language LISP; they appear on the first two pages of the book!

> If you want to communicate with a computer, you must have a way to communicate. A man mainly uses a language, such as English, to talk to another man. He can also use grunts, sighs, and a variety of more or less obscene gestures. To communicate with the computer, we use programming languages. These languages serve the same purpose as English does for communication between men. . . .
>
> If you travel in a foreign country, you are certainly better off with a partial knowledge of the local language than with no knowledge at all . . . even though a native speaker may say "razor blade" when you say "piece of metal to cut the hair on the side of my head." You may have plenty of time and can wait to learn the foreign language perfectly before saying anything in it, or you may be in a hurry to shave or, for that matter, cut your mother-in-law's throat. It's a question of priorities.
> —Laurent Siklossy, *Let's Talk LISP* (Englewood Cliffs, NJ: Prentice Hall, 1976)

The male author of this book clearly intends his remarks to be witty, to add levity to what might otherwise be dry material. He even adds a footnote commenting on what he takes to be his humorous use of generics in the first passage: "Our subject being a language of communication between a human being and a machine, we do not feel obliged to include considerations about the communication possibilities among more than two men, or between a man and a woman, or among two or more women."

But by the time we reach the next page and the second quoted passage, the joke is over. The author has lost control of his deliberate use of the generic, since he says that "you" might call a razor "a piece of metal to cut the hair on the side of my head." The "you" here clearly excludes women from the intended readership.

And the remark about cutting "your mother-in-law's throat" is unequivocally offensive even if it is intended as humorous. Imagine if the example had concerned the definition of the word *rope* and the author had suggested that you might be in a hurry to "lynch a Negro." No one in this day and age would publish such a line in a college textbook. And if it did appear, it would arouse immediate indignation and protest. Every time a pejorative comment about women appears in the required or recommended reading for a course, students are confronted with an insulting and potentially damaging lesson about women.

We have looked at a spectrum of problems, ranging from subtle forms of differential treatment of women and men in the classroom to instances of highly offensive remarks in classrooms and textbooks. All of these are part of the hidden curriculum often offered in the college classroom. Because it is hidden, and is not part of the curriculum explicitly addressed in the classroom, raising issues concerning it in an academic setting may generally be considered inappropriate. Women who express their concern about the hidden curriculum may be considered "unprofessional" or may be criticized for introducing emotional or subjective considerations into an objective, impersonal matter.

For a related reason, professors may find it hard to alter certain elements of the classroom experience that contribute to the hidden curriculum. The conventions governing the selection of primary text material are set by the official curriculum, and attempts to alter them may be seen as detracting from that curriculum. And changes in deeply entrenched speech patterns may be seen as distracting.

The hidden curriculum is a significant part of the college experience and should always be an appropriate topic for scrutiny and revision in an academic setting. And conventions can be changed. The following section explains how to begin such changes.

Solutions

One way to assess the effectiveness of the hidden curriculum being taught in your classes is to think about your own attitudes toward classes taught by women, or fields considered "women's fields." Do you tend to prefer or to avoid classes taught by female professors? Do you tend to assume those classes will be less rigorous? Less serious? Do you tend to assume that the professor will have less to contribute than a male professor? Do you generally place more stock in your work when it receives praise or a high grade from a male professor than a female one? Do you think of traditionally male fields, such as physics, mathematics, or economics, as more serious or important than fields considered more appropriate for women, such as art history, psychology, or women's studies? How often have you listened uncritically to a derogatory or belittling remark about a class taught by a woman, about women professors generally, about classes or fields where women predominate, or about womens' colleges?

Your judgments concerning what is worthwhile, valuable, and most serious may be informed by the lessons of the hidden curriculum. In addition, since the hidden curriculum teaches you certain things about your own talents and capabilities, it may encourage you to pursue certain of your options and to drop others, in a way that is not necessarily in your best interest. Exactly how this works will vary from school to school, class to class, and, particularly, from department to department. An engineering program, for instance, in which relatively few women are enrolled will present different sorts of obstacles to the female student than, say, a sociology program might present. *Remember: the hidden curriculum cannot be identified by any single rule, but it is characterized by differential treatment of women and men.* Therefore, you must be prepared to consider each of your classes independently when assessing the real curriculum being taught.

Before we proceed, a word of caution is in order. You are at college to receive an education in the official curriculum. Your efforts to combat the hidden curriculum should never take up so much time and energy that your studies suffer as a result. You will find that the techniques offered here can, with a little concentration on your part, be applied to your classroom experience on a day-to-day basis with minimal interference with your studies. In addition, insofar as the hidden curriculum may be adversely affecting your studies now, you should find that your efforts to counteract its effects result in an increased self-esteem, self-confidence, and consequently a more productive educational experience.

Developing Awareness of the Hidden Curriculum

Let's begin by reconsidering the problem Anna was having making presentations in her management class. Remember that the professor was systematically, if unintentionally, undermining the self-confidence of the women in the class. We looked at a number of different ways in which professor-student interaction in the classroom could produce this effect. Although the professor's behavior may be key in teaching the lessons of the hidden curriculum, the effects can be completely undone without changing the professor's behavior.

The first step is simple: by reading this chapter you've already taken it. This may not seem dramatic enough to you, but *simple awareness is the first crucial step toward overcoming the effects of the hidden curriculum*. The reason for this is also simple: the hidden curriculum is taught by means of behavior that distinguishes between women and men as separate groups, but in order for the lesson to be effective each individual must interpret the lesson personally. That is, to be effective, the lesson must be interpreted as reflecting some aspect of the individual's talents or capacities.

You will not learn to feel incompetent in a subject merely because a professor treats women in general as incompetent. You learn to feel incompetent when you interpret the professor's behavior as a response to your own incompetence. As soon as you learn to recognize when the hidden curriculum is being taught, you are in a position to know that the professor's behavior is not directed at you personally, and is not earned by any particular lack of talent on your part. And as soon as you come to this realization, the professor's behavior will cease to be an effective pedagogic device of the hidden curriculum.

Anna was able to recognize the hidden curriculum, even though she didn't have a name for it. We already noted that she was not inclined to interpret the professor's treatment of her as reflecting any shortcoming on her part. Her ability to perceive a *pattern* to the professor's behavior helped her maintain this view, since she noticed that women as a group were being treated differently than men as a group. For many women, recognizing that the behavior is *not* a reflection on them personally is difficult. But it is a skill that can be readily learned.

Take notice of what's going on in the class. When you feel slighted or frustrated, ask yourself why. Did the professor ignore you? Interrupt you in mid-sentence? Respond to your question in a belittling way? Pay attention to what happens when other students talk in class. Does the professor deal with women and men differently?

Be critical of your own perceptions. If you feel incompetent in one of your classes, or leave class feeling dissatisfied, or dread going to class, ask yourself why. It may be that something is going on in that class that you've taken as a sign of your own inadequacies, but that is in fact part of the hidden curriculum. Pay attention to how the professor behaves when listening to women and when listening to men. Does the professor make eye contact with the women? With the men? Does the professor look attentive when listening to the women? While listening to the men? Review the ways in which professors may communicate the hidden curriculum listed in the ''Problems'' section, and see how many of them you can spot in your classes. Once you start paying attention to these issues, you may find ways the hidden curriculum is communicated that haven't been mentioned here. And you'll find that once you get used to looking out for these things, they needn't be too distracting during class or take your attention away from the content of the class discussions.

The same sort of point applies to Consuela and Diane as well. Consuela and Diane were being asked certain sorts of questions in their classes, while other sorts of questions were being reserved for male students. As soon as Consuela feels frustrated by the question she is asked, she should ask herself why. Was the question too simple? Did it not give her enough of an opportunity to express her views? She should start paying attention to the way in which the professor calls on people to answer questions. Does the professor frequently ask simpler, more factual questions of the women? Are more abstract and complex questions frequently directed to men?

Diane too should be asking these questions. Why is she apprehensive about being called on? Why is she relieved to be asked a simple question calling for a short answer? Why does she become more and more comfortable in her education class? Is it because she doesn't think she's smart enough or well enough informed to answer more demanding questions? To what extent is the professor's treatment of her encouraging her to hold this view of herself?

As Consuela and Diane begin to look out for patterns in the classroom treatment of women, they may observe some different ways in which the direction of questions can teach the hidden curriculum. For instance, one particular professor may make a habit of addressing especially difficult questions to women during class. If the students have a hard time answering them adequately, those who are called on may feel incompetent. And even though the women may not be aware that it is a pattern, they may still automatically come to expect to be called on when they hear the professor phrasing an especially difficult question. This can create an atmosphere in which the women have reason to feel more apprehensive about going to class than the men do. But as soon as they recognize the pattern to the professor's behavior, they also realize that any difficulties they may have in answering questions addressed to them stem from the level of complication of the questions, not their own incompetence or stupidity.

Observing Your Own Behavior
Earlier examples showed how the hidden curriculum may teach women to present themselves differently in classes than do men, and in Fay's case, the student's behavior—speaking in a tentative, unconfident manner—may have contributed to the perception that she was not a competent student. Thus her own behavior may be part of a counterproductive pattern.

Women may tend to speak in the classroom, as a rule, *as if* what they were saying were not important. This style of speech may in turn be interpreted by others in the class as a cue that what is being said is less important than it might otherwise seem. Since men tend to adopt a more assertive style of speech in the classroom, as if what they were saying were important, a pattern is created that contributes to the general conception of women as in some ways lesser students.

But Fay's style of speech in the classroom is something that she can change if she wants to. We say "if she wants to" because whether Fay *ought* to change this behavior is a personal matter. Often certain sorts of assertive or brash attitudes are rewarded by commanding attention and esteem, while certain sorts of deference or humility fail to command either attention or esteem. But this does not mean that Fay should cultivate brashness above humility, for two reasons.

The first reason is a practical one. In a social setting in which deference is considered an appropriate attitude for women to express, women may tend to adopt a deferential style in order to meet with social acceptance. That is, while brashness may be rewarded in a male student as indicating ambition and intellectual vigor, in a female student it may be considered abrasive and obnoxious. Accordingly, brashness in a woman may be punished with loss of esteem.

The second reason why cultivating an aggressive style is not necessarily a good way to address this problem is that the mere fact that some pattern of social behavior is rewarded does not mean that that pattern of behavior is *good*. It may seem to you that a student should display some humility in asking questions and making comments in class. If you pay close attention to the behavior of the men in your classes, it may seem to you that their classroom behavior is often arrogant. Thus the behavior being rewarded may not coincide with behavior that you value. In fact, studies indicate that women's "style" in the classroom may be more conducive to a generally fruitful educational environment for all students than is the typical male style.

Learning to be confident in your own abilities is important. Learning not to sell yourself short in presenting your ideas or asking questions is important. But the best way to learn these things may not be by emulating the men. On the other hand, you must assess the degree to which your patterns of speech in class may be reinforcing a lower self-esteem. The more visible students—those who tend to speak more in class and make themselves heard—are certainly more likely to receive high grades and to be known by their professors, increasing their chances of being singled out for special appointments or other educational advantages, such as better letters of recommendation for graduate and professional school or for employment. Therefore, it is important for you to see to it that your style in class is not an unnecessary hindrance to your studies, no matter what style you settle on as most comfortable for you. Fay has to assess her own behavior, and make some decisions about whether and how to change it.

The first step she can take in this direction is to pay careful attention to her behavior during different classes. Does she tend not to speak at all in some of them? Is this because she really has no questions or comments, or because speaking in these classes is simply too uncomfortable? When she speaks, does she tend to speak very quietly? Does she tend to preface her remarks with apologies or disclaimers no matter what she's saying? Does she tend to give question intonation even to declarative sentences? She should pay attention to the "style" that the other students are using and to the attitude that the professor adopts in responding to these various styles. Are there other students who speak the way she does, and does the professor respond to them differently in any way than to students who speak more assertively?

Changing Your Behavior in Class

We've been speaking up to this point about *recognizing* patterns of behavior that contribute to the hidden curriculum: patterns of the professor's behavior, patterns of the students' behavior, and patterns of interaction between professors and students. As soon as you begin to spot these patterns, you can begin changing them. Now that Anna, Consuela, Diane, and Fay are aware of the patterns in their classes, they are in a position to begin changing them. Just as the patterns themselves are often made up of small gestures or comments, *changing* the patterns can also be accomplished by small gestures or comments which do not require you to be distracted from your studies.

One very effective way to change your own experience in the classroom is by making a point of *supporting other women in class.* For example, if you are in a class with Fay and a man interrupts her mid-sentence, you might raise your hand when the man is done talking and say, "Could we please return to the question that Fay was asking; that's a question that I had, too." If you don't know Fay's name, you can turn and ask her for it when you are called on, then use it. Or, when following up on a question or comment made by, say, Anna, you might make a point of crediting her by name. For instance, you might say, "I'd like to follow up on Anna's comment that. . . ." If you notice that a woman in the class has had her hand up for a long time without being called on, you might also try to catch the professor's attention and point out that she has been waiting to speak for some time.

What sorts of interventions are called for and how often you need to undertake them depend entirely on the particular patterns in your classes. Bear in mind that it is not only women who speak quietly or shyly who may need support from other students. Some women may speak assertively and confidently and still have trouble getting called on or given credit for their remarks.

You will find that your support is not only helpful to the other women but that it will be very good for you as well. The difficulties that the other women face in the classroom are the same difficulties you face. As you come to their assistance in overcoming them, you both increase your awareness of the patterns in your classes and at the same time you enhance your own ability to assist yourself in overcoming them. It won't be long before you find yourself saying, for instance, "Excuse me, I wasn't finished yet and I'd like to return to my question."

Furthermore, even without any explicit discussion, you will find that others begin to follow your example, for instance, by assisting a student who has been interrupted in getting the floor back. This

may well be true of both women and men in class. The other students may not notice when a woman is interrupted or ignored. Your
intervention points out to them what has happened, and once they
begin noticing, they too may begin intervening. The same may well
be true of your professors. In this way, without saying a word about
it, you can be teaching all the people in your classes to change the
hidden curriculum.

Organizing to Combat the Hidden Curriculum
In classes or fields where these sorts of patterns are a particular
problem, or anywhere where there is sufficient interest among two
or more women, you can organize somewhat more formally along
the same lines. Together with one friend or a group of women ac-
quaintances, you can arrange to lend each other support in the classroom.

When you work as a group, you can divide up the tasks. For instance, some women in the group may be very shy, and others
bolder. You might want to assign the bolder women the task of assisting in getting the floor back after an interruption, since this task
may sometimes call for a bit more forcefulness, or a willingness to
make repeated attempts. A quieter woman might want to take on
the task of steering the class discussion back to a question previously
asked and ignored. But experiment a little. You may find that in
some classes, the best way to get other students to quiet down and
listen to a point is by having a student from your group who doesn't
speak a lot, and who tends to speak softly, make the point. If she
speaks quietly, then the others must be quiet in order to hear her!

If you have a few friends who are interested in this sort of thing
but you don't have any classes together, that's not a problem. Each
of you can make an effort to intervene in the ways we've been talking about in her own classes, and then you can meet from time to
time to compare notes on what you've learned about the patterns in
your classes, what sorts of interventions are easy and effective, and
which ones other students pick up on quickly. Comparing notes on
different classes and different fields gives you perspective on the patterns you see. And discussing your efforts at intervention in your
classes with other women trying to intervene in their classes gives
you support and perspective on your own experience.

Every action you take to change the patterns of classroom behavior that teach the lessons of the hidden curriculum contributes to
what we might call a *counter-curriculum:* one that counteracts the
hidden curriculum. This counter-curriculum teaches people to take
women seriously as students and can be an effective educational

tool. Anna, Consuela, Diane, and Fay can start teaching the counter-curriculum in their classes immediately.

We haven't discussed how Fay can change her habit of speaking hesitantly and apologetically in class. But if she makes an effort to support other women in the ways we mentioned, she may find that changing her own habits comes naturally after a while. She can also make a concerted effort to change her habits, by pure force of will. Toward the end of this section, we're going to discuss other ways in which working with groups of women can be useful, and we will recommend some specific techniques for helping one another undo bad habits. You can also modify some of these techniques for use on your own. So if you want to change some classroom habits of yours, and you're finding it difficult to do so by sheer willpower, don't worry! We're going to return to this matter in a little while.

Learning New Speech and Thought Patterns

We talked in the "Problems" section about how ordinary language in the classroom could contribute to the hidden curriculum by fostering stereotypes and an exclusion of women. Here's a little test you can perform to see whether the use of masculine terms and stereotypes has been having an effect on you.

In class lectures, in textbooks, and in your own thoughts, you often come across descriptions of people in stories that do not specify gender, or you hear names of scholars, artists, or scientists whose gender you don't already know. Next time you encounter one of these characters or names, try to picture the person under discussion as quickly as possible, and with as little reflection as possible. Do you picture the person as a man? If you picture the person as a woman, can you think of a special reason for this? Is the character a member of a stereotypical women's profession or field? A nurse or a teacher? A patient or an invalid? A dependent or subordinate relative to others in the story?

If you automatically imagine the character as a man, then try picturing the character as a woman. Is this difficult or uncomfortable? If it is, why? If you tend to picture as men all hypothetical characters and people you hear or read about whose gender you don't already know, and if you tend to make exceptions for certain professions, occupations, or characteristics, then the language you hear and use every day is having an effect on you. It is contributing to a way of thinking that may make your inner, mental world populated almost entirely by men.

In the college classroom, having your inner world populated mostly by men can interfere with your education and your ability to con-

sider all of your options for what you study and what you will do
after college. Since the sorts of speech patterns we are talking about
teach the hidden curriculum by affecting your views and conceptions, the trick to undoing the lessons they teach is to find some way
of changing those conceptions. The message of the hidden curriculum is being passed on in these cases by certain uses of language, so
we can change the message by changing the language.

This may seem an intractable problem, since you can't very well
change the ways in which other people speak. But the interesting
thing about this problem is that in order to beat it *all you have to
change is your own speech.* With a little practice, you will find that
simply changing your own use of language in small ways will be
enough to create an effective counter-curriculum for yourself.

Simply make a conscientious effort to use feminine terms in hypothetical examples where you would have used masculine terms in
the past. For instance, if you want to make a point about a hypothetical anthropologist, try saying, "When an anthropologist is classifying artifacts, what she has to do first is to. . . ." And make an
effort to avoid terms like *mankind,* saying, rather, for instance, *hu-
mankind.* Pay special attention to avoiding the sort of stereotyping
by gender that we discussed in the "Problems" section. If you want
to give an example involving an executive making a hiring decision,
for instance, make a point of referring to the executive as *she.*

You can also presume a feminine identity when talking about a
real person whose gender you don't know. For example, if someone
is telling you about the first head of medical services at your college
and you want to know the person's name, you could ask, "What was
her name?" After all, if it seems more "natural" to ask for "his"
name, this is only because the *presumption* is that the first head of
medical services was a man.

Forcing yourself to presume that the person is a woman, or to use
feminine terms in generic contexts, has three different effects. In the
first place, practicing this policy for even a short time will teach you
a great deal about the ways in which your own patterns of speech
have been affecting your ways of thinking about the world. Every
time you use a feminine term in one of these ways, you will immediately and clearly be aware of how strong your presumption used
to be that the person under discussion was male.

Second, forcing yourself to change the language you use *in spite of*
those presumptions will lead you to give them up. The new use of
words will bring with it a change in your conceptions. And it won't
be long before it's just as easy for you to think of a hypothetical

anthropologist, or member of any other profession, as a woman as for you to picture the person as a man.

Third, your new pattern of speech will help create a counter-curriculum for those around you as well. After all, their inner worlds are also populated largely by men, and your speech will serve to make them aware of this fact. You may find that after a while your new mode of speech will be contagious. Students and professors alike may begin to change their old ways of speaking.

This new speech pattern may seem awkward to you at first. But you have to keep in mind that any departure from an old custom seems uncomfortable and awkward in the beginning. If the old custom is a damaging or unproductive one, then the temporary discomfort of changing it is always worth the effort. We recommend this particular change in habit also to those of you who may be skeptical about how big an effect the use of generic masculine terms can be having on you. Try our recommendation for at least a little while. Since it takes some getting used to, you should allow yourself at least four weeks of conscientious attention to your language in order to see any effect. You may not be able to feel the effect of your old habits of speech on you now, but if you change them for a while, we guarantee that you'll feel the effects of the new ones. And we suspect that you'll like them.

Needless to say, everything we have said here applies to the use of forms of address as well. Make a point of referring to female scholars by last name alone, as you do for male scholars. Do not refer to a woman as "Ms." in circumstances in which you would refer to a man as "Professor" or "Doctor." Changing habitual patterns of address that contribute to the hidden curriculum will have an effect analogous to that of changing patterns of generic terms.

Getting "Included" in Class
After the discussion in the "Problems" section about the generic and stereotypical uses of gender-specific terms, we looked at a couple of specific examples of ways in which professors' remarks or jokes can contribute to the hidden curriculum by excluding women. Once again, the first and crucial step in counteracting the hidden curriculum when it is taught by such remarks and jokes is to become aware of the messages that are being conveyed. As soon as a remark is made that makes you uneasy, you should be prepared to give yourself the benefit of the doubt: there is probably a good reason for your discomfort.

When the joke about the hourglass shape was made in Gina's

physics course, Gina probably experienced something like embarrassment or self-consciousness. She should not attempt to convince herself that she is too sensitive or too sheltered. There is a very good reason why the joke has an immediate and unpleasant effect on her. As soon as she begins to understand why, she will be in a position to fault the professor correctly for the remark, and not fault herself for her response to it.

Gina has to be able to say to herself, "That joke was offensive," or, "The professor's remark is inappropriate." She will then stop taking it personally, and jokes like that will cease to become effective pedagogic tools of the hidden curriculum.

One thing she might consider is making a comment in class at the time the joke is made. She might say, for example, "That joke is insulting to the women in the class, and carries the implication that you are only talking to the men." In the "Solutions" section to Get Smart Course 202 we will discuss useful ways to express yourself when discussing such matters with professors whose behavior is causing you discomfort. At this point, we return to an issue mentioned in the "Problems" section, namely, that the hidden curriculum is generally not viewed as appropriate matter for discussion in the regular curriculum.

It is likely that Gina would be uncomfortable making such a remark during class, and also that the professor's response might not be supportive or sympathetic. For this reason, we do not suggest that Gina feel obligated to intervene at the time the joke is made. However, if Gina feels so inclined, she should speak up. No matter what the professor's response, it is almost certain that other students in the class who would not have given the matter any thought at all will perceive the offensiveness of the joke as a result of Gina's comment. In this way, Gina has the power to intervene directly in the teaching of the hidden curriculum. At the same time, she may find it personally satisfying to have spoken up immediately.

If Gina would be uncomfortable raising the matter during class, she might prefer to speak to the professor after class and explain in a direct manner why the joke made her uncomfortable. Once again, we refer you to the "Solutions" section of Get Smart Course 202 for some tips on making such a discussion fruitful. While the other students may miss the immediate benefits of Gina's remarks, it is possible that the professor may understand Gina's discomfort once it is pointed out, and avoid such jokes in the future. Also, it may be good for Gina herself not to let the matter go without comment.

Either of these options would be completely appropriate and useful, but it is entirely up to Gina to decide whether she would be comfortable exercising them. There is also something else she can and should do. Immediately after class Gina should seek one or more of the other women in her class to discuss the matter with. Or, if there are no other women in the class, or if she feels too uncomfortable speaking to them, then she should find a friend, preferably a woman, to discuss the matter with. She may find that in conversation she and her friends are able to gain a perspective that would not come easily to her on her own. Even if all that is discussed is the joke itself and the fact that it made Gina uncomfortable, talking with other people who also find the joke offensive is the best cure for its likely effects.

This point cannot be stressed too strongly: *Talking about problems of this sort with other women is one of the best ways to combat the problems.* Discussion heightens your awareness of the nature of the problem. It lends you support and perspective on the problem. And in the course of discussions, you may invent new and more effective ways to make college more productive for yourself and the women around you. Perhaps as a result of conversations Gina may have with other women in her class, a few of them will decide to talk to the professor together. Or perhaps the professor's remark will be the occasion for Gina and her friends to form a plan to support one another during class.

Dealing with Offensive Remarks and Sexist Texts
If a professor's behavior is creating a real problem for the women in the class, and if the professor does not respond appropriately or adequately when approached on the matter, then it may be wise to approach the Chair of the professor's department, or the Dean of Students for assistance. You might also want to speak with your campus Ombudsperson, or the Affirmative Action Officer. (See the "Solutions" section of Get Smart Course 404 for an explanation of the various campus administrative offices which might be of assistance in such cases.) This would be the case with "jokes" of the sort Gina heard in class, particularly if the professor treated the objections of Gina or others in an offhand or offensive manner. This is also the case with the problem of offensive textbooks, such as the LISP book we quoted in the "Problems" section.

When you come across offensive passages in textbooks that you are required to read for a course, you should bring the passage to the attention of the professor. For any course that uses a textbook, there will be several competing texts on the same subject. If the one being used is offensive, it should be a simple matter for the professor to switch texts at least for future semesters.

By the way, if you are trying to convince a professor that a passage in a textbook is offensive, and if the professor is having a hard time seeing your point, then it is often useful to do what we did in discussing the LISP text: try rephrasing the passage so that the remark pertains to blacks or Jews, while changing as little of the original content as possible. Many people are more sensitive to racist or anti-Semitic remarks than to sexist ones, and this ploy may help you convince a skeptic that the passage is offensive.

The problem of primary texts that contain offensive passages is a different matter. There is not much that you as a student can or should do about the official college curriculum, although you should take every opportunity to raise issues concerning the biases of primary texts during your classes, and to rectify omissions of women from scholarly consideration. You can also make a systematic effort to seek out women scholars, artists, and scientists to write about or talk about when you have the opportunity. There is a growing literature on the contributions of women to world history and culture. Browse in your local bookstore or library or subscribe to one of the women's book review journals (such as *Women's Review of Books* or *Belles Lettres*) to keep up-to-date.

It is quite possible that your college has a women's studies program, or that courses stressing the accomplishments of women are offered. A complete listing of women's studies programs in the country is published annually in *Women's Studies Quarterly* (The Feminist Press). We strongly recommend that you seek out and attend courses of this sort. It will have a generally therapeutic effect, since in the rest of your classes you may practically never hear about the contributions of women. But in addition, perhaps particularly in fields that especially interest you, you will find that exposure to the great women in the field—and there have been great women in virtually every field—will have an enormous beneficial effect on your sense of your own potential for being a serious worker in the field.

Working in Groups to Outsmart the Hidden Curriculum
Let's turn now to ways in which you can work together with other women to undo the lessons of the hidden curriculum. One thing that a group, even a small group, of interested women can do is to undertake a consciousness-raising campaign. You might organize a "teach-in," for example. Depending on the number of people interested in organizing it, and the size of the crowd it is intended for, you might choose a single afternoon session or a series of sessions. You could invite people to give talks or conduct discussions that might focus, for example, on women scholars who are neglected in

the standard curriculum. Or, they might focus directly on the problems of women students on your campus. You could invite someone from the women's studies program at your college or a nearby college to talk about women in certain fields. You might invite someone from the local Women's Center to lead a discussion among women of the problems they experience in classes. A panel of students might prepare a short talk about the problems of women students in the classroom, and then hold an open discussion of the issues. Certain sessions may be good consciousness raising for the faculty, too. You might be able to get department Chairs to encourage faculty attendance. You might also be able to find sources of student funds to invite speakers from outside the campus community. Rooms are generally available on campus for just such sorts of meetings, particularly if you meet in the evenings. Check with the Student Union, Student Activities board, or Dean of Students for information specific to your campus.

In conjunction with a teach-in, or independently, you might want to do a small sociological study of your college or of a particular department. This can be done without interference with your studies. You may find the sample chart on page 32 useful for such a study. You could take a chart of this sort to your classes, and keep running tallies on the various aspects of the hidden curriculum that we've discussed. Or your group could divide up the task, with each of you taking tallies in certain classes or on certain days. In this way, you can collect a great deal of information without any one person taking too much attention away from her studies. When something noteworthy occurs, you need only make a little check mark on your chart or jot down a word or two of description. This chart is only one example. You might want to design a chart that addresses your particular concerns, or one intended for use in classes that are particularly problematic. If you are in a science program, you might want to make up special charts for laboratory sessions. It is important to keep a separate chart for each course.

The results of a study conducted with such charts could form the basis for a session at a teach-in. You might have the women who took the tallies present and discuss them, and then invite everyone to join in a discussion of what can be done about the problems you have found.

By the way, these tallies can also be put to a number of other uses. At the end of the term when you are filling out course evaluations, you will be able to comment on specific problems you experienced as a woman in the class and what their mechanism was. This kind of information can be very important to professors. Since your re-

CHARTING THE HIDDEN CURRICULUM: Familiarize yourself with the incident categories on the left-hand side so that when one occurs in class, you can simply put a stroke mark in the appropriate box. For example, each time a woman is called on in class, put one stroke mark in the "Female student" column of the category "Is called on by professor." You may also need to add a few words to fit your class experience, and you may want from time to time to jot down a few notes or remarks from class that you think are particularly characteristic or revealing of the class situation.

Course name Professor	Female student	Male student
Asks question or makes comment		
Is called on by professor		
Is interrupted		
Interrupts another speaker		
Is referred to		
Uses generic masculine terms		
Professor's manner of speaking to student:		
Interested		
Attentive		
Serious		
Disinterested		
Casual		
Offhand		
Student's manner of speaking to professor:		
Deferential		
Apologetic		
Hesitant		
Questioning		
Quiet		
Loud		
Assertive		

Additional remarks:
sexist jokes, offensive behavior, other notable incidents

marks will be specific, they will assist the professor in taking steps toward correcting a problematic situation.

Another thing you might do with the tallies would be to write a letter to the editor of your campus newspaper. Or your group might want to write an article on the problems you have uncovered, or to persuade someone who works on the paper to write such an article based on your data. Ask for responses from readers.

Creating Alternative Educational Settings

Another way that a group of women can reverse the lessons of the hidden curriculum is to create alternative educational settings. You might organize, for instance, a one-day women's conference on campus. You could solicit papers in all fields from women undergraduates, and encourage women students and professors to attend presentations of the papers. The conference could be organized just as many professional conferences are run, with different papers being read to small groups throughout the day. Chances are that many more women than men will attend; you may find that the preponderance of women makes it easier to present papers, and also that there is a completely different style—a more constructive style—to the discussions of the papers in this setting.

Or, along the same lines, you might have a monthly meeting for women in a particular department, or in the college as a whole, at which a woman student could present a paper or lead a discussion in a subject she is working in, or where you could simply pick themes for group discussion at each session. These sessions could be organized as social events as well, with refreshments. Particularly if you are interested in meeting as a group of women in one field or area of study, you might consider contacting the women graduate students, if the field has a graduate department on your campus. They might be interested in collaborating on such a program, or on any of the other programs we have suggested.

Among other things, an ongoing group of this sort to which faculty are invited provides a way for women to gain visibility with their professors, something men tend to have an easier time doing in a coeducational environment. Such a group forms the basis of a network of women on campus that can serve many valuable functions.

Consciousness-Raising and Assertiveness-Training Groups

From time to time you might invite women scholars from other schools, or feminists, to talk or to lead sessions. Some sessions of such a group might serve as general consciousness-raising or assertiveness-training sessions as well. You can use these sessions to help one another develop more constructive styles, by encouraging one another to speak up and to avoid overly deferential or hesitant ways of talking.

Here's an experiment that the members of your group might want to try. At one meeting, you could discuss the ways in which your own styles in the classroom might be contributing to the hidden curriculum. Then, each of you who is interested in participating could pick out one aspect of her own behavior that exemplifies what you've been talking about. For example, Fay, who expressed herself with apologies and disclaimers when she spoke in class, might pick her tendency to preface her remarks with apologies. Diane, who was shy and avoided speaking in class, might choose her tendency to avoid asking questions.

Each of you could then agree to change that one aspect of her behavior in the class that is most problematic, for some fixed period of time. If your group is going to meet again in three or four weeks, then the time between meetings would be perfect. By the end of the initial meeting, each member of the group should have chosen the behavior she wants to change and should have a concrete plan for doing so.

For example, Fay might focus on her tendency to preface her classroom remarks with apologies or disclaimers. She picks one class in which she speaks fairly often and in which she is aware of engaging in this practice regularly. She gives herself the task, for the chosen period of time, of never allowing herself to preface a remark in this way. When her impulse is to begin a question with, "I'm sorry, but is this point related to what we were discussing before . . . ?" she should simply drop the opening apology and say: "Is this point related to what we were discussing before?"

Diane might focus on her unwillingness to speak in classes at all. She chooses the class in which she feels she would be least at ease in asking questions. Diane then sets herself the task, for the chosen period of time, of preparing one question in advance of each meeting of the class, and seeing to it that she asks the question before the class is over. Another student might decide to ensure that no one succeeds in taking the floor away from her when she is speaking. Someone else may want to eliminate her use of masculine terms.

If you have a hard time envisioning in concrete terms how you will go about changing the aspect of your classroom behavior that you have chosen, discussing this with the group should help. As a group, you may be able to come up with useful strategies. The particular task you have chosen for yourself may be uncomfortable to perform at first. It may help to remind yourself that you are performing an experiment for a fixed amount of time in a chosen class. Think of the experiment as a sort of acting lesson, or a game.

At the next meeting of the group, or after the chosen period of time is up, the group members should discuss their experiences during the experiment. Each of you stands to learn a tremendous amount about how your own behavior influences your classroom experience; about ways in which your behavior "cues" other people to respond to you in certain ways; and about the ways in which your behavior affects how you think of yourself and what you have to say. Some of you will have found that after a few classes, the task you had given yourself came easily, and was even pleasurable. Some will have had more difficulty or received disconcerting responses from professors and other students. By discussing the results of your experiment in the group, you will all gain perspective, support, and a great deal of insight into the way classroom interaction teaches both hidden and counter-curricula.

At the end of the chosen period, you can always return to your old style if you want to. But because you will have forced yourself to cultivate a style of behavior quite different from the one you were used to, you now have a *choice* that you did not have before concerning which style you adopt. You may like the new you, and decide to continue and extend your new classroom image. You may settle on some style intermediate between your old one and your experimental one. Or you may decide that you really preferred yourself the way you were originally. In any case, your behavior is no longer determined by the hidden curriculum, but is a matter of your choosing among options you have given yourself.

This experiment is something you can perform on your own, too. We recommend trying it as a group so that your experiences can be discussed with others engaged in the same sorts of tasks, but it can be just as effective if you try it alone. Or in a more informal group. You and a friend could try it. Or you could try it alone, and then talk over your results with a friend or two.

Particularly if you commute to college or attend an urban college without a real campus, finding other women in your school to talk with may be a problem. Try posting a notice on some prominent school bulletin boards that you are interested in forming a women's group—a consciousness-raising group, a group to organize a teach-in, a study group, or simply a social group. This can be very fruitful in many ways. And if you feel a desire to meet women to talk with about these things, there will no doubt be other women who feel the same way. You might also drop by the local women's center, where there will almost certainly be other women who share your concerns.

We've given you several suggestions for ways to start working immediately to install the counter-curriculum as a permanent fixture on your campus. And by reading through other chapters in this book, you will find further suggestions for activities and techniques that can be fruitfully applied to the problems of the hidden curriculum. To conclude, we repeat the two central lessons of this chapter.

First, *be critical of the hidden curriculum.* Learn to recognize when it is being taught, and learn to say no to its lessons. Be critical of your own attitudes toward the activities of women, because they may already reflect the lessons of the hidden curriculum. If you think of a class taught by a man as more serious than a class taught by a woman, ask yourself why. If "men's" and "women's" classes or fields are different, are the men's classes necessarily better? What is it that you value? What is it that interests you? And what is the hidden curriculum trying to teach you about those values?

Second, *take every opportunity to speak about your experiences and concerns with other women,* either informally with a friend or two, or in organized groups. All women are being taught the same lessons, although each individual will register them in different ways. The perspective and support you receive from other women may be the single most effective means of deflecting the lessons of the hidden curriculum. And in the course of talking, who knows what other ideas for improvement you may come up with? The authors of this book know this from firsthand experience—after all, it's as a result of talking with each other and with other women that we got the idea to write this book!

Solutions Summary

- Recognize when the hidden curriculum is being taught; learn to spot patterns and not to take them personally.
- Learn to monitor your own style in class.
- Support other women during classroom discussion.
- Organize with other women to provide mutual support during classes.
- Point out offensive remarks, and comment on them to professors and to other students.
- Pay attention to language; try changing your own use of masculine terms.

- Pay attention to stereotyping; don't stereotype people by gender.
- Seek out women scholars to write about and discuss; investigate women's studies courses given at your college.
- Report offensive behavior to the appropriate administrative offices.
- Organize teach-ins.
- Set up alternative educational settings, such as occasions for women to present papers or one-day conferences for women.
- Take tallies of student-professor behavior in your classes.
- Form groups for assertiveness training and networking among women students and faculty on your campus.

Above all, be critical of the hidden curriculum, and take every opportunity to talk with other women about what goes on in the college classroom.

Get Smart
Course 202

Faculty-Student Relations:
Working with Your Professors

Student-professor relationships are a key element of college education. They can offer lessons to the student on nonacademic subjects, too. Relationships with male professors can serve to instruct the female student in maintaining a subordinate status within the college community. The result of this is something we call **the upstairs-downstairs effect**.

Since most professors are men, the upstairs-downstairs effect can have a strong influence on the college experience of women. Difficulties with these relationships can also create obstacles to a woman's academic education. In the "Solutions" section, we'll teach you how to control the effects of difficulties with professors. We will also begin teaching you techniques for intervening on your own behalf when a professor's behavior presents you with an obstacle to your academic progress.

Problems

Interaction between students and professors is an important part of any college education. Get Smart Course 101 discussed student-professor interaction in the classroom. But students and faculty often interact outside the classroom as well, casually in brief exchanges on campus, in occasional meetings during professors' office hours, throughout extensive research projects, and socially at receptions, cultural events, and parties. When the student is a woman and the professor is a man, even the most casual interaction can easily become complicated and, from the student's point of view, damaging. This chapter focuses on the problems women face as students trying to get along with their male professors.

The Upstairs-Downstairs Effect
Starting off with the mildest sort of problems and working our way toward extreme cases of sexual harassment, let's begin by accompanying a hypothetical student to her Asian Studies Club meetings.

> Helen is an Asian studies major and a member of her college's Asian Studies Club. She's the only woman of the seven students in the club, and Professor Hopper, who chairs the club's meetings, is a man. Helen participates actively in the club's activities, is friendly with the other students in it, and feels generally accepted, at ease, and productive at club meetings. But from time to time Professor Hopper asks her to run little errands, such as getting coffee or doing photocopying; he never asks any of the other students to do these things.

Helen is in some ways flattered to be given special tasks, and she really doesn't mind at all being helpful. But she begins to notice that she has bouts of insecurity about her own abilities to do worthwhile work and about her seriousness as a student. These bouts of insecurity follow fairly regularly two or three days after she has been sent on one of these errands.

Helen's ambivalent feelings are quite understandable. Her experiences exemplify a common theme in the experiences of women in higher education, which we call the *upstairs-downstairs effect*. The name is borrowed from the television serial whose title refers to the two realms in a well-to-do British household: that of the gentry, the upstairs realm, and that of the gentry's servants, the downstairs realm. The two realms are well integrated, with the servants playing a key role in upstairs life, but always in such a way as befits their status as servants. Relationships can be better or worse between any given servant and any given member of the employer's family, but the role each plays in the relationship is governed by the distinction between servant and employer.

The female student is, of course, not a servant to a professor, but male-female relations sometimes have an analogous dynamic in our society. This is certainly the case on the college campus, where men may be considered primarily as participants in the intellectual life of the university, but where women may be perceived and treated as if they were primarily girlfriends, wives, or people biding their time until marriage. In short, women are often treated as people who naturally have the function of supplying social support for men, and who participate in the intellectual life of the college community only in a special and limited capacity. Even while feeling fully integrated into college life, the female student may find that those around her perceive their relationships to her as governed by the distinction between women and men. Consequently, she will be constantly reminded that she is perceived as a denizen of the "downstairs" world. *An event has the upstairs-downstairs effect when it calls the student's attention to the difference in status between the male professor and the female student and reminds the student of her downstairs (low status) affiliation.*

In learning to recognize this situation, remember that *the hallmark of the upstairs-downstairs effect is ambivalence.* Here's how it works in Helen's case. Professor Hopper probably doesn't think twice about asking Helen to run these little errands. They seem to him to be perfectly innocuous tasks. And from Helen's point of view, they do make her feel like an important and contributing member of the club. Nor does she perceive each request at the time it's made as inappropriate or offensive. In some respects Helen enjoys the special status they give her. However, the cumulative effects of the errands take a toll on her as she feels increasingly uncomfortable and uncertain of her role in the club.

The tasks Helen is asked to perform are tasks that would normally be given to the secretarial staff, such as photocopying, including those that shouldn't be given even to the secretarial staff, such as going out to get coffee for the faculty. It's no accident that the men are not sent on similar missions: Professor Hopper would not be so at ease asking them to do secretarial tasks, because he would immediately perceive this as inappropriate. Both he and Helen have to some extent been socialized to think of women in a way that makes these requests of Helen seem appropriate. The message Helen receives is clear: she is not like the other members of the club. There is something about her that makes her more suited than her male peers to secretarial tasks and errands.

Helen is indeed "upstairs" a good deal of the time with the rest of the Asian Studies Club. Professor Hopper's attentions in some ways integrate her into the club, and she takes pleasure in being singled out and given special tasks to perform in connection with the club's operations. At the same time the underlying message is loud and clear that Helen really belongs downstairs, and is only upstairs by special dispensation. Every time she is asked to go on one of these errands, Helen is being told that she's a natural-born photocopier or procurer of coffee. This is a classic example of the upstairs-downstairs effect.

The upstairs-downstairs effect can be produced by any number of casual requests or remarks. For example, since a woman's appearance is often considered her most important characteristic, professors may routinely, often in a sincere attempt to be kind, compliment a female student on her dress, her new hairstyle, or even her legs. If you are ever served such a compliment and you find yourself disquieted by it, don't fault yourself for oversensitivity. Remember the upstairs-downstairs effect! The compliment may be flattering, since it conveys approval from the upstairs community; but it also suggests that your appearance is what the professor is marking as important. This sets you apart as one of the downstairs denizens.

Any remark that calls attention to the student's gender may have the upstairs-downstairs effect. For example, a professor might comment on the difficulties you would face in your studies if you were to become pregnant. Or, a professor might express some prejudicial ideas about women, such as their being more likely to want babies than to be serious about their careers or their being too emotional to be counted on. Any of these sorts of comments can abruptly remind the student that she is being set apart as a member of a special group. Sometimes the student may have the sense that such a remark is made as a sort of test, to see how far she can be pushed or to make her acknowledge her downstairs status.

Social Situations
Let's turn now to another type of situation. Isabella has a problem that looks a little different from Helen's, but it has a similar effect on her sense of her own abilities and seriousness.

> Isabella has requested an independent study in mathe-
> matics with Professor Ingers, who is a man. Isabella and
> Professor Ingers plan to meet one day at noon to discuss
> their plans for the semester's work. Isabella arrives on
> time at Professor Ingers's office with books and a pro-
> posed outline. Professor Ingers suggests that they discuss
> things over lunch.

Isabella's immediate reaction to the suggestion is confusion. While she arrived at Professor Ingers's office eager to discuss what she thought was a very solid proposal for her work, he has introduced a social element into their meeting for which she was not prepared. After a moment's hesitation Isabella agrees to go to lunch. On the one hand, for a student to be asked to join a professor for lunch is extremely flattering, and on the other hand, Isabella is immediately unsure of what his real intentions were in agreeing to supervise her independent study. The double edge to Isabella's reaction—flattery on the one hand and alarm on the other—should immediately sug-gest to her that she is experiencing the upstairs-downstairs effect.

Isabella must now consider the possibility that Professor Ingers is interested in her sexually instead of, or perhaps in addition to, being interested in supervising her work. When Professor Ingers agreed to the independent study, Isabella took it as a sign that he thought of her as a capable student. Now she questions whether he cares about or has even bothered to evaluate her work at all. Even if the con-versation over lunch goes exactly the way Isabella would have ex-pected it to go in Professor Ingers's office, the mere fact of its happening over lunch leads Isabella to doubt Professor Ingers's real interests and, by extension, her own worth as a mathematics stu-dent. The introduction of the social element into the work relation-ship automatically produces the upstairs-downstairs effect. A male student in this position could naturally interpret the lunch invitation as a sign that he is someone whose company Professor Ingers enjoys, and this would bolster his sense of himself as a serious student. Isabella immediately senses that the invitation to participate in the upstairs life may be based on the professor's perception of her not as a mathematics student but as a woman. Isabella's confidence in herself and in her mathematical abilities is undermined as a result.

The fact that the invitation produces the upstairs-downstairs effect on Isabella even when it may have been genuinely innocent is not due to Isabella's paranoia or insecurity: it is due to the social situa-tion itself, which is as a matter of fact more complicated for her than it would be for a man in a similar position. It's easy to see how repeated invitations from Professor Ingers for lunch or coffee, or to meet with him at odd hours of the day, will lead Isabella to be increasingly unsure of his interests and of her own abilities.

Antisocial Situations

Isabella's discomfort at the first meeting is not only expected and understandable, it turns out to be a warning sign fully justified by what actually transpires over lunch.

Professor Ingers takes Isabella to the Faculty Club, puts her books and outline on an empty chair, and proceeds to ask Isabella a number of questions concerning her social life, her cooking abilities, and her plans to have children. There is no discussion of the outline Isabella has prepared for the independent study.

Isabella criticizes herself afterward for not having attempted to steer the conversation to her outline. In fact, she looks back with shock at the fact that she was friendly and cooperative and answered all of Professor Ingers's questions, instead of confronting him directly with the inappropriateness of his questions, or simply walking out. Her principal recollection of the conversation in retrospect was that she had felt muddled and dull-witted throughout it, as if she were attempting to think with her head full of dense fog.

This foggy feeling is a very common symptom of the upstairs-downstairs effect in situations like Isabella's. Isabella started the day preparing to plan her semester's advanced study in mathematics and ended up answering a professor's questions about her cooking and child-rearing plans. For many reasons, Professor Ingers carries great authority for Isabella. He is older than she, he is a professor, and, not least of all, he is a man. Since he has set the tone for the lunch conversation, he clearly thinks that his questions are appropriate. Isabella doesn't come into his office seeing things the way he does, but it is very difficult for her to maintain her tenuous sense of herself as a serious student in the face of this authoritative insistence that she is someone with whom child care, cooking, and dating are suitable topics of conversation—someone with whom a professor doesn't consider discussing mathematics at all.

Isabella's relationship to Professor Ingers becomes extremely complicated the moment Professor Ingers begins to ask his questions, and the confusion she experiences during the course of the lunch is a direct reflection of the complexity of the situation. It takes a great deal of experience and encouragement, probably particularly for women, before one is able to maintain one's own preferred image of oneself against such weighty opposition.

In addition, while Isabella was genuinely appalled by her professor's behavior in retrospect, at the time of the lunch her impulse was to appease rather than to confront. In part, this impulse is a deeply ingrained effect of the socialization of women in our culture, but in part it is a pure self-preservation tactic. In fact, these two things tend to go hand in hand: in a culture where women are supposed to be compliant, compliance becomes a necessary tactic for their social success.

In one respect, Isabella is lucky. Professor Ingers's conduct is so crude that Isabella may be able to recognize fairly easily that something is amiss in his treatment of her. Many situations are not so clear-cut. A professor may ask you out for coffee, but then proceed to discuss your work with you just as if you were in his office. This is no problem in and of itself, provided you learn to recognize and counteract the upstairs-downstairs effect. He may suggest lunch, and then intersperse talk of work with friendly small talk about innocuous subjects. Perhaps he will suggest talking over drinks or dinner. A professor may suggest that you go for a walk, or join him in attending a lecture somewhere. Each of these possibilities is confusing for the female student, and almost invariably produces discomfort and ambivalence. It is open to question whether the professor is indeed making sexual advances, or preludes to sexual advances, by any one of these invitations.

The crucial point is that *there is ambiguity in every one of these situations by virtue of the fact that the professor is a man and the student is a woman.* And so at the very least, no matter how innocent the professor's intentions may be—and this is not to suggest that they always are—the very occurrence of a situation that evokes the upstairs-downstairs effect serves as a reminder to the student that she cannot for one minute think of herself as merely a student among students in the college community. The student is also, and in some cases first and foremost, a woman, and she will be singled out accordingly. Once again, the student's sense of herself is diminished. The extremely high incidence on college campuses of male professors pursuing sexual relationships with their female students additionally warrants the student's apprehensions.

Consensual Professor-Student Affairs

The discussion so far has assumed that a student would not welcome sexual advances from a professor, but this may not always be the case. Even under the best of circumstances, however, problems will arise for the student who eagerly gets involved just as easily as for the student who doesn't. Consider Jean's case:

Jean willingly becomes involved with Professor Jim Jaffe. The relationship itself is a source of satisfaction to her. In addition, since Jean has begun going to social gatherings with Professor Jaffe, she finds that her relationship to other faculty members has become more friendly and collegial. Jean would like to go to medical school, and she asks another professor of hers, Professor John Jackson, who has been particularly sociable with her since her involvement with Professor Jaffe, for a letter of recommendation. One evening, in the course of casual conversation, Professor Jaffe says to Jean, "By the way, John called last night. You'll be glad to hear that he was just sitting down to write your letter of recommendation." When Jean asks whether Professor Jackson wants to speak to her, Professor Jaffe says, "No, he just called to chat. We talked a while about how I feel about the prospect of your going off to medical school next year." Jean starts to ask something further about what Professor Jackson said. She stops short. For the first time since she has become involved with Jaffe she feels acutely uncomfortable addressing Professor Jackson as "John." On the other hand, saying "Professor Jackson" seems equally awkward. Rather than use either form of address, Jean changes the subject.

Jean's discomfort is produced by her sudden ambivalence. Why is she confused about what to call Professor Jackson? A careful review of her conversation with Jaffe will give us the answers. Being involved with Professor Jaffe has enabled Jean to perceive herself as a peer with faculty members. She's become accustomed to calling them by their first names. When this dialogue begins, Jean is aware of feeling particularly close and collegial to both Professors Jaffe and Jackson. After all, they are expressing concern for Jean's future not just as her professors but as her friends.

When Professor Jaffe mentions that he and Jackson discussed his attitude toward her application to medical school, Jean is suddenly uneasy. Did Professor Jackson really call to speak with Professor Jaffe about Jean's application? What did Jaffe say, and could what he said have affected Jackson's letter of recommendation? The conversation between Jaffe and Jackson seems to have been quite casual. But to Jean it seems as if the consequences for her future could be serious. Not only does Professor Jackson have a certain amount of power to affect Jean's future, but it seems that Professor Jaffe, simply by virtue of his involvement with Jean, shares this power. Does Professor Jackson think that Professor Jaffe's preferences are relevant? Jean feels left out and dependent.

This ambivalence between feeling like a peer and feeling like a dependent is a sure sign of the upstairs-downstairs effect. The confusion is immediately reflected in Jean's inability to choose between the form of address she would choose as a colleague and the form she would use as a subordinate.

In fact, Jean's apprehensions are warranted. Even under the best of circumstances, where neither professor thinks that Jaffe's preferences should influence Jackson's letter, Jackson may not be aware of the ways in which the tone of his conversation with Jaffe can influence the letter he subsequently writes. If Jaffe were not involved with Jean, it is conceivable that Jackson would have asked Jaffe for his professional opinion of Jean as a student. But the question of Jaffe's personal preferences for Jean's future would not have arisen. Merely by becoming involved with Jaffe, Jean has extended the influence that Jaffe *as a professor* has on her future. The cause may be their closeness as peers, but so long as Jaffe is a professor and Jean is a student, one of the effects is an emphasis of their inequality.

This one episode does not cause Jean's feelings toward Professor Jaffe to change substantially. And in fact, she still enjoys the opportunity to socialize with faculty that the relationship brings with it. But now when she goes to faculty parties, or has friendly chats with professors between classes, she always feels a strange sense of discomfort and a new and exaggerated sense of being subordinate. In some ways Jean's involvement with Professor Jaffe may be as reciprocal as any. But, for Jean, the mere fact of its being a student-professor relationship means that it has the upstairs-downstairs effect. Jean enjoys all the privileges that come with the relationship, but she is often reminded that she receives those privileges solely by virtue of Jaffe's patronage.

Remember, the key ingredient of the upstairs-downstairs effect is ambivalence: there has to be some taste of upstairs life in it for the student to nibble at all. A professor's advances hold out many promises to a student: the prospect of genuine acceptance by someone whom the student admires; the possibility of entering a relationship with this person as a peer; and what may appear to be the student's best chance to be "accepted" as a peer. Of course, there is always the possibility that any two people will be simply genuinely attracted to each other. But the point is worth stressing that even in cases where the professor's attentions are truly welcomed, and where mutually desired sexual relationships develop, the full force of the upstairs-downstairs effect may still be felt. It may be a sad reflection on the culture we live in, but a male professor–female student love affair can never be an innocent matter, even in the rare cases in which on balance it takes no real toll on the student's capacity to achieve a rich and fulfilling life for herself.

Sexual Harassment

Another important aspect of student-professor relationships to consider involves situations in which the professor makes explicit sexual advances that are unwelcome by the student and that carry an implicit or explicit threat if the student does not cooperate. These are the cases that are usually referred to as *sexual harassment.*

Kim's case is a classic example of this behavior.

Kim has applied for her college's study abroad program. She is an excellent student, and seems to have a very good chance of being accepted into the program. Furthermore, one of the professors on the committee that makes the acceptance decisions seems to like her and think highly of her work. Shortly before the decisions are to be made, this professor—a man we'll call Professor Kline—calls Kim into his office. He closes the door behind her and then attempts to kiss her. When Kim pushes him away and expresses her disgust, Professor Kline becomes angry. He accuses her of having "led him on" in order to secure a place in the program, and tells her that she had better go through with what she started if she still hopes to be accepted. As Kim turns to leave his office, Professor Kline tells her that if she tells anyone about what has happened, he will see to it that she is accepted into neither this program nor any special program she may apply for in the future.

Kim is naturally quite flustered and upset, to say the least. When she gets back to her room she begins to go over the episode in Kline's office, and certain themes keep running through her head. She wonders why he said what he did about her having led him on. Was it true? Had she been flirtatious with him? Did she in fact try to charm or perhaps seduce him into favoring her for the year abroad? Did she possibly owe it to him to do what he wanted if he was going to get her into the program? If she hadn't flirted with him, what had she done to provoke his behavior?

In addition to figuring these things out, Kim must decide whether she should tell anyone, and, if so, whom. On the one hand, Professor Kline's threats are alarming, and he seems to have the power to change substantially the course of her education if he so chooses. On the other hand, Kim wonders what damage he can do if she doesn't report it and get someone to prevent him from affecting the decision. Then again, if she doesn't report it, perhaps he will recommend her for the year abroad after all, just so that she doesn't accuse him publicly of having harassed her. And even if she wanted to report it, who would believe her if he denied the incident?

The "Solutions" section will devote full attention to Kim's options. But we will stress one vital point here: *No matter what Kim may or may not have done prior to the incident in Professor Kline's office, she is not responsible for his actions; Professor Kline has no right to abuse the power he has as a participant in decision making about Kim's future to force her into sexual relations with him.* Kim needs to stop worrying at once about her role in the whole thing, or about her obligations to Professor Kline. He has behaved in a way that cannot be justified, certainly not by anything that Kim may have done. His action is unconscionable. In fact, it is illegal.

Nonetheless, even if Kim presses charges against him and he is indeed held legally accountable for what he has done, Kim has already been subjected to a very potent manifestation of the upstairs-downstairs effect. Notice that this time the ambivalence is not between pleasure and discomfort so much as between anger and guilt. Kim has been graphically reminded of the special vulnerability she has as a woman in college, and of how tenuous her standing as a good student is.

The definition of sexual harassment is often extended to include not only cases like Kim's, where both sexual advances and the threat of retaliation for noncooperation are explicit, but also cases in which either the advance or the threat is implicit. This would cover those cases, such as Isabella's discussed earlier in this chapter, where there is no explicit sexual advance but merely some amount of sexual innuendo. And the term *sexual harassment* can also include cases in which there is no sexual advance, but where something is said or indicated that pertains to the student's gender and adversely affects her educational environment. In this broader sense, it is clear that this entire chapter has been devoted to sexual harassment.

Kim's case makes painfully plain a set of social circumstances that

work their way back to and shade into Helen's case. These circumstances clearly make relationships with male professors difficult and
sometimes damaging for the female student. *Do not let anyone tell you
that you are too sensitive when you get confused about a simple social gesture
from a professor. Take your confusion, or anger, or ambivalence seriously:
you are not imagining things.* You are simply responding to those aspects
of your college environment that produce the upstairs-downstairs effect. This effect can be undone and your environment can be changed.

Female Professors and Male Students
You may be wondering why we haven't discussed similar complications in relationships between professors who are women and students
who are male, or between professors and students of the same sex. Of
course, complications may arise in these cases, but they are far less
serious as a rule. That is, any one particular affair may be quite serious
in its implications for the student, but there is no comparable problem
for these students as a class. There are several reasons why these kinds
of cases do not tend to be as difficult as male professor–female student
relationships.

The first reason is that, because the great majority of college professors are men, the male student who is having trouble with a particular
female professor can easily afford to alienate her, or to turn to another
professor for assistance in straightening things out. It is not as simple
for the female student to explain to a professor's male colleagues that
the professor is making unwanted advances.

Second, male students may have other ways of becoming accepted
by professors as colleagues, or at least as prospective colleagues. Therefore they are not as vulnerable as women are to being pulled into a
sexual relationship with a professor in order to obtain acceptance.

Third, the male professor–female student configuration adds a very
powerful hierarchical dimension—the male-female dimension—to an
already hierarchically defined relationship. The female professor lacks
this additional social clout.

And the fourth reason is that men are socialized to hold their own,
and to stand by their sense of their own worth, more readily than are
women. Therefore they will have less difficulty in extricating themselves from uncomfortable professor-student relationships. Men are
thus much less vulnerable than are women to the mere appeal of being
sexually desired by someone in a position of authority.

Similar considerations apply to relationships between professors and
students of the same sex. The general point is that in order for the
upstairs-downstairs effect to occur, there has to be an upstairs for the
student to be excluded from and a downstairs to be included in. Stu-

dents and professors may be temporarily unequal, but the inqualities are in principle transitory and short-lived. The case is different with women and men, and so the problems of male professor–female student relationships are different from the others.

Solutions

Since this chapter has discussed a wide range of problems, a number of different sorts of remedies will have to be considered. A review of the cases presented in the "Problems" section offers an opportunity to see what options each of the students had in her particular situation.

In the first case, Helen was experiencing the upstairs-downstairs effect as a result of being sent on certain errands for her Asian Studies Club, which left her feeling unsure of her abilities and seriousness as a student. Helen has two principal problems to solve: first, how to overcome the upstairs-downstairs effect and prevent her situation from undermining her self-confidence; and second, figuring out what she can do to change the situation.

Overcoming the Upstairs-Downstairs Effect
There are two steps to overcoming the upstairs-downstairs effect: you must learn to recognize it when it occurs, and you must learn to counteract it. Recognizing it is fairly straightforward, and we have already pinpointed its hallmark: ambivalence. The upstairs-downstairs effect may involve ambivalence between pleasure and unease, between anger and guilt, between a sense of power and a sense of subservience, or between a sense of competence and a sense of incompetence. *Whenever you experience ambivalence either as a result of or in the course of interaction with a male professor, stop and ask yourself the following questions:*

- *What is it that I like about the situation?*
- *What is it that I dislike about the situation?*
- *How would things be different if I were a man?*

Consider how Helen would answer these questions. She suspects that she is experiencing the upstairs-downstairs effect as soon as she notices that she both likes and dislikes being sent on these errands by Professor Hopper. In order to be sure that this is the upstairs-downstairs effect, Helen asks herself the three questions.

What is it that she likes about the situation? She enjoys being useful and feeling like an integral part of the Asian Studies Club, insofar as she is providing some service necessary to its activities.

What doesn't she like? Helen doesn't like the sense of being singled out for these tasks for the wrong reasons. Helen doesn't like the sense that somehow the professor, and possibly the other students, think that the tasks are what she is fit for. Above all, Helen doesn't like feeling that her contribution to the Asian Studies Club consists of the errands instead of something else, and that she is not good enough to be a serious student.

How would the situation be different if she were a man? Since none of the men in the club are sent on these errands, Helen suspects that the situation would never occur at all were she a man. But even if the situation did arise, Helen suspects that if a male club member were singled out to do all of the errands, his response after a while would be annoyance. He would probably soon complain loudly and clearly about his treatment. When she thinks about it, Helen doubts that the errands would give him any pleasure at all, and she doesn't think that they would make him doubt himself the way she is doubting herself.

In other words, Helen doesn't think that the situation would arise were she a man, and she doesn't think that a man would like the same things or dislike the same things about the situation. Therefore, Helen correctly concludes that she is definitely experiencing the upstairs-downstairs effect.

Any ambivalence produced by a situation that would either not occur or not produce ambivalence were you a man is the result of the upstairs-downstairs effect.

You owe it to yourself to take all signs of the upstairs-downstairs effect seriously. The upstairs-downstairs effect may seem trivial in some of its occurrences, but it is one of the most pervasive and damaging mechanisms of discrimination against women: it causes their self-confidence to be undermined, affecting their judgments about the course of present and future education as well as other aspirations and employment plans. And the upstairs-downstairs effect contributes to barring women effectively from a large number of social relationships with professors that are important to success in higher education and the working world.

Now that Helen has recognized it, counteracting the upstairs-downstairs effect will not be that difficult for her. However, it may take her a little time to perfect the technique that follows, and to learn to use it consistently. The main idea is simple. What the upstairs-downstairs effect does is to remind you that you are considered and should consider yourself a woman first and a student or scholar second. In addition, it serves to remind you that women are only secondarily included in the educational system at all. The trick to beating the upstairs-downstairs effect lies in refusing to accept these messages.

Sounds simple enough, right? But Helen still needs to know how she's going to do this. *Helen needs to pick a few well-chosen sentences designed to restore and support her self-esteem, and then to rehearse them to herself from time to time.* For example, since the errands make her doubt her own seriousness as a student, she chooses the sentence, "I am a serious student." Since she is indeed a serious student, repeating this line to herself a few times reminds her that it is true. Or again, since it is the Asian studies professor who is sending her on the errands that make her uncomfortable, she says, "It is Professor Hopper who is doing things that make me uncomfortable." This sentence correctly identifies the person responsible for the problem, and does not allow Helen to tell herself that it is something about her that makes these errands her task.

Helen must repeat these lines to herself whenever she begins to doubt her own seriousness and abilities, a few times before going to club meetings, a few times when leaving club meetings, and again as soon as some task is assigned to her. If she does this, she will find that the errands annoy her, but that after a very short time they no longer produce the upstairs-downstairs effect. This is because Helen is no longer allowing Professor Hopper's assignment of her to the downstairs realm to be her own assignment. Repeating these lines to herself allows her to rise above the image of her that his behavior suggests, and to hold on to an image of herself that she chooses, one that allows her to continue with her studies with a strong sense of her own abilities.

Changing Helen's Situation

What can Helen do to change the situation? The first thing that she has to do is to define that aspect of the situation that she would like to change. She should pick something small and manageable. If she decided, for example, that the real problem is that men don't take women seriously as scholars, and that this is what she would like to change, she will not be able to achieve her goal! *Pick a task that can be easily stated, that is immediate to the problem, and that will positively affect the immediate situation once it is accomplished.* Helen's problems stem immediately from the errands she is sent on, so she picks as her task to get the professor to stop sending her on them.

How she goes about performing this task will depend greatly on her particular situation. Helen might want to consider how she would go about turning down a similar sort of request made by a friend or peer. Perhaps the next time Professor Hopper asks Helen to perform one of these tasks for the club, she might say, "I did the photocopying the last few times, perhaps someone else would like to do it this time." Chances are that this is all it will take.

If not, Helen should remember that some of the men in the club might have already noticed that the professor is treating her differently, and some of them may think as she does that this isn't good. Depending on the extent of her friendship with them, she might want to mention the matter to one or two of them and see if they agree with her. It is always nice to have encouragement from those around you. It might also be that Professor Hopper is genuinely unaware that he is treating Helen in any way inappropriately, but that if it were pointed out to him he would be sensitive to the problem and quick to change his behavior. Again, Helen must judge to some extent what sort of response he would be likely to give. The most direct approach would simply be for Helen to tell him that she is uncomfortable running these errands.

This could be tactfully done alone after a club meeting, or perhaps in the company of one or two other sympathetic club members if that would be easier for Helen. *The key to success here is to be direct and tactful at the same time.* Indirection or talking around the issue only leads to confusion, and will leave Helen feeling ultimately dissatisfied with the discussion. A lack of tact may well put the professor on the defensive, causing him to turn a deaf ear to what he might under better circumstances have listened to quite earnestly.

In this context, it is common to make the distinction between being aggressive and being assertive. *You're being aggressive when you directly accuse another person of obnoxious or offensive behavior. You're being assertive when you directly point out what it is in the situation that makes you uncomfortable.* You're being neither if you either say nothing at all or say things that don't or only partially reflect the truth.

Helen decides that she would like to talk to Professor Hopper alone. So one day after a club meeting she asks if she could speak with him. It just so happens that on this particular day he did not ask her to do any errands. That doesn't matter. Even if he had sent her on an errand only once, talking to him would still be important and justified. In fact, since it is quite difficult to sort out the various factors in the upstairs-downstairs effect on the spot, it is often necessary and legitimate to respond some time after the problematic situation has occurred.

When Helen and Professor Hopper are alone, she sits still for a moment and collects herself. She silently repeats to herself her chosen sentences, "I am a serious student," and "His behavior has been making me uncomfortable." Then she proceeds to explain to him as directly as possible that when she is asked to do the photocopying or to go for coffee, she begins to feel as if she is really only good for this sort of errand, as if such tasks are the only contribution to the Asian Studies Club that she is capable of. She tells him that she doesn't think he is deliberately trying to make her feel bad, but that she wants him to know why it makes her uncomfortable.

In Helen's case she is lucky. Professor Hopper thinks over what she has said, and replies that he is sorry that she has felt this way and that he will try not to do things that make her feel uncomfortable in the future. If he accidently does so, he asks her to tell him immediately so that he will be aware of it and stop what he is doing. As Helen leaves the room she repeats to herself, "I am a serious student, and a success!"

In other cases, one might not be so fortunate. Although generally if you are assertive and not aggressive you will get a relatively sympathetic answer, the professor might not change his behavior at all. Or, the professor may tell you that you're too sensitive and emotional, hence confirming his worst fears about women as students. In this case, you have a few more options that you can try. One option is to find another faculty member whom you think will be sympathetic, perhaps a woman, and to ask her to talk with the problematic professor. Another option is to find out if any other students are having problems with the same professor. If so you can talk to him as a group, remembering to be assertive and not aggressive. Sometimes numbers can convince.

If in the course of your conversation with the professor he says anything to you that is offensive, threatening, or inappropriate, you should consider reporting this to the Dean of Students at your college or to the Chair of the professor's department. For example, if he tells you that you're lucky that he lets women in the club at all, or that if you insist on being difficult he'll expel you from the club, then you must seek recourse with the Dean, the Chair of the department, or some other campus official.

Finally, the last option is that you can simply refuse to do the errands any more, independent from whether the professor understands or approves. In that case you may incur his anger, but again, if he gives you a hard time, you should consider talking to the department Chair or the Dean of Students about it. The professor is acting in this case, once again, way out of line.

Of course, there is one other option in Helen's situation, which really is the first one to consider. This is simply to say nothing and to continue running the errands. We do not recommend this course. In the first place, the more women start objecting to inappropriate treatment, the faster change will come about. But more important, it will become increasingly difficult for Helen to enjoy her studies as she builds up resentment at her treatment. Eventually she may either succumb to the image of herself being suggested by the tasks, or simply decide that the whole thing is not worth the aggravation, and leave the club.

But the Asian Studies Club may be of paramount importance to Helen. And if she is convinced that both Professor Hopper and the other students would be entirely unsympathetic to her objections, and that they would become angry and self-righteous were she to complain, then Helen might choose to stay in the club and continue the errands. In this case, it is even more important than ever that she rehearse her lines as often as possible. She should also add the line, "It is my choice that I do this errand." It is important for Helen to remember at all times that she has a choice. No one is forcing her to do the errand; she has decided that it is the best course. The minute she begins to resent running the errands, she should stop.

But, as we said, Helen was lucky. She talked the situation over with Professor Hopper, and they worked things out. We leave her busily and happily pursuing her studies, and only having to nudge the professor from time to time to be more sensitive.

By the way, the difference between aggressiveness and assertiveness can be the key to success in many different situations. As mentioned in the "Problems" section, many kinds of remarks can produce the upstairs-downstairs effect, and when these remarks are made in your presence you may feel "put to the test." Assertive, nonaggressive, responses can often enable you to "pass" these tests. For example, if a professor makes a remark to you about women not being serious or reliable, you could say, "I am serious and it makes me uncomfortable that you might assume that I'm not just because I am a woman." Or, if a remark on your appearance makes you uncomfortable, you could say, "It makes me uncomfortable to have my appearance commented on since I want to be judged like all other students on the basis of my work, not my appearance." A professor's response to such a remark may often be, "I had no idea that you're so sensitive!" or, "Women just can't take a joke!" Don't let such responses bother you. They carry the implication that you've overreacted to the original comments, that there never was a test to begin with. But there was a test. Therefore, such remarks are the clearest indications you can have that you've passed the test with flying colors. Under the circumstances, what else could the professor say?

Isabella's Lunch Problem
Now let's turn to Isabella's problem. Remember, Isabella wanted to discuss her independent study plans with Professor Ingers, but when she got to his office he suggested that they have lunch together and then proceeded to ask her about her marriage plans and other personal topics.

Isabella knows from experience that when she goes to talk with a professor, she is often a bit muddleheaded, and often realizes what she should have said or done only after the meeting is over. She also knows that this is a common symptom of the upstairs-downstairs effect. So before her meeting with Professor Ingers, she repeats to herself a few times, "I am a serious student." But in spite of this precaution, the very first sentence that Professor Ingers utters throws her into a state of confusion. And so she *immediately* repeats to herself, "His behavior is putting me in a difficult position," before she has time to distort the situation by wondering what she has done wrong. By the time she agrees to lunch, just moments later, she is once again composed, and knows that Professor Ingers has done something to make her feel uncomfortable but that she needn't take it as her problem.

When they get to the Faculty Club and he begins to ask his questions, Isabella is once again acutely uncomfortable. As soon as she becomes uncomfortable, she should remind herself of those things that the situation is trying to make her forget. It may help to repeat them silently to herself in the course of the discussion. So she adds a couple of new lines to her repertoire: "Professor Ingers is making it very hard for me to work with him," and "He shouldn't be putting me in this difficult position." In general, anything that lets you rise above the situation and remember that no matter what the professor may think you do not have to follow his rules will do the trick. Isabella does not have time to go through the three key questions in detail during her lunch with Professor Ingers. Thus, the option she chose of reinforcing herself through the repetition of her chosen sentences was very good. In this way she was able to maintain some perspective on this incident with Professor Ingers while it was happening.

One of the very important steps that Isabella has already taken is to recognize right away that Professor Ingers's questions are inappropriate. Helen too was able to be clear on this point, at least upon deliberation. You need to be able to recognize when a professor's behavior toward you is inappropriate and to hold the professor, not yourself, responsible. Ask yourself, for example, Is his question an appropriate question for a professor to ask a student? Or, Would the professor talk this way to a man? If the professor's behavior is in any way inappropriate, or in any way makes you uncomfortable or confused, then the professor is failing as an educator. Do not seek to hold yourself responsible. Do not wonder whether you belong in college after all. Do not ask what you did to bring this about. *Remember: you are a serious student, and you do have a right to equal educational opportunity. If a professor is in any way interfering with this right, then the professor is out of line. Nothing you have done can justify the professor's behavior.*

Isabella is already in a good position to deal with her situation, because she has resisted the upstairs-downstairs effect. Now let's see what she can do about the situation. In the first place, she had an option as soon as Professor Ingers suggested that they talk over lunch: she could have refused. If the prospect of talking over lunch truly upset her, and she felt that it would be more productive to remain in his office, then she should have said so on the spot, once again being assertive and not aggressive. This decision is one that Isabella must make for herself. In such situations it is very important to follow your instincts. Isabella could simply and directly have said, for example, that she would be more comfortable talking in the office and preferred not to talk over lunch. Professor Ingers might have accepted this at once, but he might not have. How far Isabella wanted to push her objections, or argue her position, would depend on the strength of her feelings about the matter and her judgment of the professor's intentions. But the point is that Isabella already has a choice: she does not have to go to lunch with him.

Isabella chooses, however, to go with him to the Faculty Club. This is an entirely acceptable choice. After all, an invitation from a professor for lunch is flattering, and holds out the prospect among other things of a fruitful working relationship. Certainly no one would blame a male student for accepting such an invitation; it might even be considered frivolous to decline. And since Isabella has no way of knowing in advance what Professor Ingers really has in mind, or in any event no more than a nasty hunch, she decides to give him the benefit of the doubt. Her having accepted the lunch invitation in no way makes her responsible for what happens next. Even if she comes to feel afterward that she showed bad judgment in giving this particular man the benefit of the doubt, his behavior is in no way justified by her misjudgment. It is very important for Isabella to keep this in mind at all times.

So they go to lunch, and Professor Ingers begins asking intrusive questions. Isabella now has several options. From the very first question he asks her, she need not wait to see whether things get worse or whether he will indeed turn to academic matters. She can tell him right away, for example, "If you don't mind, I'd like to talk right away about the independent study," or, "I'd prefer not to talk about personal matters, can we get to the independent study?" No matter what response Professor Ingers gives, his questions are inappropriate and Isabella need not answer a single one of them. He is asking about things that are truly none of his business.

The chances are that if Isabella responds immediately and directly in this assertive manner, Professor Ingers will not persist with his questions. On the other hand, it may be that Isabella will have to repeat herself several times before he really gets the message. It may even be that Professor Ingers refuses altogether to desist, and becomes angry when she proves uncooperative. This is not very likely to happen, but if it does, Isabella should not feel obligated to remain polite. She should repeat to herself, "His behavior is inappropriate and offensive," and be prepared simply to leave if he refuses to turn to an appropriate subject.

Notice that Isabella has the option of responding aggressively to Professor Ingers from the very first question. Insofar as his behavior is offensive, it is entirely appropriate for her to be angry. She can tell him right away, "Your behavior is offensive," and then get up and leave. Strong responses to offensive behavior can sometimes be good for the soul. Isabella must judge for herself the consequences of an aggressive response, but if she is so inclined, Professor Ingers's behavior certainly warrants her anger.

Isabella does not choose an aggressive response, in part because she has worked very hard on her independent study proposal and it is very important to her that this particular professor oversee the semester's work. In addition, she fears that alienating him may cause serious problems for her studies in the future. Being aggressive in this way may very well alienate Professor Ingers. For this reason, as long as Isabella values his academic assistance, it may not be the most practical avenue. Nevertheless, Isabella is kidding herself if she thinks that merely by remaining polite she can continue to work fruitfully with this professor, particularly if he does not change his behavior when she objects to his questions. In such a case, working relations with Professor Ingers will never be good: Isabella will be constantly apprehensive and uncomfortable. And, as would have been the case with Helen, the pleasure Isabella takes in her studies would certainly diminish as a result.

There is an important point to be made with respect to this matter of judging the consequences of standing up to a professor who is behaving badly. In the first place, it is not necessarily true that if you express anger or indignation, the professor will reciprocate with anger. This depends very much on the particular professor. You may often be surprised at how quickly a professor will back down when directly confronted with your anger. In the second place, even if your reaction does provoke anger on the professor's part, it is extremely important not to overestimate the extent of any given professor's power, or of your dependence on any one professor. We cannot stress this point enough! It is a very rare situation in which one professor has the power to influence decisions in a way that will greatly affect your future. In the course of a college education you will have many professors and many opportunities to have your work evaluated. A single bad grade, or a single negative appraisal, can seldom be a serious hindrance. *You may feel, for any number of reasons, that it is particularly important for you to continue*

*working with a professor who happens to be harassing you; but this is almost
never true. Even though it may be a real educational loss not to be able to
work with a particular professor, working relations under these conditions
can never be truly fruitful and will always eventually be damaging. There
are always other educational opportunities.* You can always find more
fruitful educational avenues than continuing a difficult working relationship with a professor who is giving you problems.

Sometimes there is no way to avoid losing a working relationship
with a professor with whom you would like to work. This may be
especially true in cases where the problems are manifested in subtle
and elusive ways, not so clear-cut as in Isabella's case. For example, if
Professor Ingers had restricted the lunch conversation to "innocuous"
small talk, Isabella might find it even harder to communicate her discomfort to him. Even if Professor Ingers repeatedly made appointments
with Isabella to work on the independent study project, but then never
discussed work with her, so long as their conversations were purely
"friendly" it is possible that neither he nor any other faculty member
would understand her discomfort or be sympathetic to her complaints.
In this case Isabella might simply have to give up working with Ingers,
even if it seems an educational loss.

Getting Assistance from Other Professors or Administrators
Any time you are denied access to someone you want to work with on
the basis of your gender, you are being wronged. It is always appropriate to take action to remedy the situation, though what sort of action
would be effective depends on the particular situation. In a case like
Isabella's, Isabella ought to consider going directly to the Chair of Professor Ingers's department, to the Dean of Students, or to any other
faculty member whom she feels would be sympathetic. She should
report the episode just as it happened. This action can serve several
functions.

In the first place, it is extremely likely that Professor Ingers has similarly harassed other students and will continue to do so in the future.
The more students who lodge complaints against him, the more his
department or the administration is forced to see a pattern to his behavior. This makes it easier to take disciplinary action against him, and
it makes it easier for other students to have their complaints taken
seriously.

Second, the faculty member or administrator that Isabella speaks to
may be able to talk to Professor Ingers directly and inform him that his
behavior is unacceptable. This form of censure may be more forceful
than any Isabella can undertake on her own.

Finally, if Isabella's grades in Professor Ingers's classes suffer as a result of her meeting with him, or if he in any way attempts to interfere with her progress in her studies, then he may be engaging in a form of retaliation. Retaliation is illegal, and the college administrator should be able to intervene on Isabella's behalf. This can happen only if Isabella calls the matter to the administrator's attention. In cases as serious as this, one can approach the Office of Affirmative Action or the Committee on Sexual Harassment, if there is one on campus. These steps are discussed in greater detail in Get Smart Courses 404 and 505.

Isabella should also consider asking other women who have taken classes or worked with Professor Ingers whether they have had any problems with him. As we said, he may very well show a pattern of such behavior. In that case, a group of two or more women may want to make a joint appointment with the dean to describe the situation. Not only is Isabella likely to find other women who have had problems with Professor Ingers, but she may also help a student who has not yet had problems but who will encounter problems with him in the future. Forewarned is forearmed, and she may be able to help the other student simply by letting her know that she is not alone.

After some reflection Isabella decides to make an appointment with a woman, Professor Isaacs, on the faculty of Professor Ingers's department whom Isabella feels will be sympathetic. Since the semester is already under way, Isabella cannot afford to drop the independent study and she needs to find a replacement for Professor Ingers. Professor Isaacs is appalled by Professor Ingers's behavior. However, she does not have time to supervise Isabella's independent study herself. The two of them decide that Isabella should talk to the dean, who arranges for another person to take over Isabella's independent study. Moreover, the dean also promises to have a talk with Professor Ingers about his behavior. Isabella writes Professor Ingers a note which reads as follows:

Professor Ingers,
I have decided to continue my independent study under the supervision of another professor. The personal nature of our conversation over lunch makes me think that I would be more comfortable working with someone else.

Although the new supervisor is not the person Isabella would have chosen to work with, the semester proceeds without further complications, and the outline she proposed for the independent study proves to have been an interesting and productive one. In addition, Professor Isaacs and Isabella decide that there should be more discussion among the women in the department. In fact, they soon begin holding informal social gatherings for women students and faculty from the mathematics department.

Isabella was lucky to find another faculty member who was sympathetic to her problem. While people's attitudes and awareness are changing, it is still very difficult for many people to recognize why Professor Ingers's behavior is a problem for Isabella at all. In addition, it is unusual to find a faculty member who is willing to take any action against another faculty member. Even administrators will tend to see things from the professor's point of view. This makes it all the more important for Isabella to be prepared to fall back on her own resources. *Independently, Isabella has the ability to counteract the upstairs-downstairs effect; the choice to sever working relations with Ingers if they become difficult for her; and, above all, the ability to talk informally (among friends) or formally (in discussion groups) with other women interested in overcoming these sorts of problems.*

Assessing Student-Professor Involvements
Next is a somewhat different set of problems, that suggested by Jean's case. Jean became involved with one of her professors, Professor Jaffe, only to find that other faculty members no longer seemed to consider her an autonomous and serious student. As suggested earlier, sexual relationships between students and professors can be complicated in a number of ways. Once involved in the relationship, there is not a great deal that Jean can do to influence the attitudes of others. She can point out to them the peculiarity of their consulting Professor Jaffe on matters that she feels are her business alone. She should certainly discuss the matter openly and directly with Jaffe.

No one can say categorically that you should never get involved with a professor. That is a very personal matter, and the decision is, of course, entirely up to you. But there are certain things you might want to consider if you are thinking about getting involved with a professor. Such relationships may seem to offer a number of rewards, but these seldom come without strings attached. It is important to enter such an involvement with your eyes open. You could start by testing for the upstairs-downstairs effect. Ask yourself the first two questions from our list: What do you like about the possibility of a relationship with this professor? What don't you like about the possibility of a relationship with this professor? Try to think through the consequences of what Jean confronted. Consider how the relationship will affect your day-to-day life. If, for example, the professor is teaching a class that you are currently taking, how will an affair affect your attitude toward the papers you write for him? Will they become more difficult? Will his criticisms be hard to bear, or will you be able to take them seriously at all? Will you always suspect that he favors you when assigning grades? Or will he tend to be harder on you in order to compensate? How will class itself go? Will you be very distracted, or self-conscious? Will you be more anxious when taking exams? Will complications arise for your education if you fight or split up? What happens if you break things off before the semester ends? Will it be reflected in your grade? All of these questions are very important. At the very least, you might consider postponing any further involvement until the semester is over, and then not taking any more classes with him.

How will the relationship affect your social life? We've already seen how Jean's social life has been complicated, even while she enjoys her new role in socializing with faculty. How will your friends view the affair? Will your friends and his friends be friends? What will it be like to be involved with someone whose friends are all older, and with whom you share only each other's company as a social life? Not to mention the enormous complications that arise if he is married.

Finally, be as clear as possible about what really attracts you to him. *A relationship with a professor may seem to offer you a certain upward mobility: it may make you feel older, more serious, more accepted as a scholar, more a part of the college community. But be careful: the only thing harder than pulling yourself up by your own bootstraps is trying to pull yourself up by clinging to someone else's.* No gain that you achieve in this way will ever be without dues. You will always have to wonder whether being attached to a man might be the only way for you to take yourself seriously, and in the end this will be destructive.

Ask yourself whether you feel smart or muddled in serious conversation with him. If you feel muddled, watch out: you may be trying to project the confident image of an established intellectual at a time when the somewhat wobbly image of an aspiring intellectual might fit you better. Ask yourself how the affair makes you feel about yourself in relation to other women, both students and faculty. If it gives you a feeling of being in any way above them, watch out: *dissociation from other women is a sign that you're experiencing superiority by association with men, and not a boost in your real sense of self-worth.*

Does he tend to belittle your academic aspirations? Does he act as if your homework is not as important as your attending to his needs? The attraction of a liaison with someone "above" you in life can be blinding. Don't overlook the little things; they may be the truest indicators of what's really going on. By the way, everything said here applies equally to relationships with male graduate students who may be teaching assistants or who may even teach courses at your college. Above all, remember that if the relationship is to work at all, it has to be a relationship between peers. This means that you and he will have to work together to counteract the undesired social and educational consequences of your relationship.

Clear Violations of the Law

The last case is Kim's. Professor Kline has engaged in an explicit and crude form of sexual harassment. Sexual harassment of this sort is against the law. Although everything we have discussed in this chapter can be considered to be within the category of sexual harassment, many problems are too subtle, too self-contained, or in other ways so constructed as to make formal action inappropriate or unproductive. Kim's case is not one of these. Professor Kline has broken the law.

It bears repeating here, because it is so important, that *nothing that Kim has said or done can in any way justify Professor Kline's behavior.* Kim owes it to herself and to other women to report Professor Kline to the appropriate authorities. Readers who have experienced problems of this sort are referred to Get Smart Course 505, in which the legal options available are addressed in detail. There are also offices at the college that are especially set up to handle such cases. The functions of the different campus offices are described in the "Solutions" section of Get Smart Course 404.

Solutions Summary

- Resist the upstairs-downstairs effect. In uncomfortable situations, ask yourself the three questions:
  1. What do I like about the situation?
  2. What do I dislike about the situation?
  3. How would the situation differ if I were a man?
- Remind yourself of your abilities and preferred self-image by using concise key sentences.
- Recognize inappropriate remarks and behavior, and hold the professor responsible, not yourself.
- Address the situation directly, bearing in mind the distinction between being assertive and being aggressive.
- Turn to others for support and assistance: other students, other faculty, and any other member of the college community whom you feel may be helpful.
- Don't overestimate your dependence on any one professor. Remember that there are many more professors and a variety of educational opportunities on your campus.
- Trust your instincts: if you think there is a problem, then there probably is one. Don't wait for the situation to worsen; address problems on the spot. If you recognize a problem only after the fact, do not hesitate to raise the issue at a later date.

- Familiarize yourself with the campus offices that can assist you, and be aware of your legal rights to equal educational opportunity.
- Organize with other women, especially in cases involving a professor who has a history of harassing women on your campus, or in particularly problematic departments.

Finally, never underestimate the value of simply discussing sexual harassment with other women, both students and faculty. Although some women will seem not to recognize what you are talking about at all, you might be surprised at how often another woman will immediately recognize a situation you describe, even one that you're not sure is really problematic at all. Remember that by the time they finish college, almost all women will have experienced the upstairs-downstairs effect. Talking it over with friends is a very good way to get a perspective on the problem and to learn how to rise above it.

Get Smart
Course 303

Decision-Making Procedures: Increasing Your Odds When Decisions Get Made

This chapter looks at the ways in which all the small educational obstacles we've discussed so far can add up to something we call the **stacked-deck effect.**

A student's academic progress is affected at numerous points during college by decisions made about her by faculty and other officers of the university. For example, decisions are made concerning the awarding of academic prizes, the assignment of on-campus employment, and letters of recommendation to graduate and professional schools. The stacked-deck effect can influence the outcomes of these decisions.

In the "Solutions" section of this chapter, we're going to add some new techniques for intervening on your own behalf when decisions are made by faculty or others that may affect your academic progress. These techniques will help you even out the odds, eliminating the stacked-deck effect.

Problems

Get Smart Course 101 considered a number of reasons why women may be less visible students than men. Women may tend to present themselves less loudly and assertively than men. Professors may tend not to call on them as frequently, not to address complex questions to them, or not to give their remarks as much attention as men's remarks. Other students may tend to interrupt them, cutting short the amount of class time in which women have the floor.

In all of these ways, students and faculty contribute to a classroom pattern in which women have lower visibility than men as a rule. This "as a rule" clause is important. Individual women may be vocal and assertive in class, and may find themselves with plenty of opportunities to make themselves heard and have their comments noted. But for the reasons discussed in Get Smart Course 101, women *on the average* may have a harder time gaining visibility in the classroom than do men.

The problems discussed in Get Smart Course 202 contribute to low visibility for women as well. A professor who works closely with an individual student has the opportunity to get to know the student and the student's work. If women have a harder time forging such ongoing work relationships with professors, then they will have fewer opportunities to gain visibility in this way.

Low Visibility and Its Consequences

The problem with low visibility is that, when it comes time for faculty to make decisions about individual students, it becomes very difficult for a student with low visibility to gain the high evaluations that swing decisions to her advantage. In some cases, it is very easy to see how this works. A professor who has not heard a student speak a great deal and has never worked individually with the student is unlikely to have formed any real opinion of the student's work, particularly in cases where the professor has seen only one paper or one or two exams of the student's. If faculty are making a decision concerning the awarding of some prize or departmental job, then a student who is "invisible" in this way to each person on the faculty has far less chance of receiving the award than a student who has even one real advocate on the faculty.

In other cases, the connection between visibility and evaluation is more complicated. Professors may tend to assume that a student who doesn't stand out in class is mediocre until evidence to the contrary is presented. Hence it may be difficult for the average woman

to raise the professor's estimation of her abilities. Since both professors and students are to some extent socialized to expect less of
women as students than men to begin with, it may even be the case
that on the average, professors tend to think less of a woman with
low visibility than of a man with equally low visibility.

In fact, studies have shown that both women and men tend to rate
the same work lower if they believe it to have been done by a woman
than if they believe it to have been done by a man. Hence, while
there will always be some women who are successful in gaining the
sort of visibility in the classroom required for high evaluations,
women may as a rule have to work harder than men in order to
attain comparable results.

A close look at faculty decision making shows how this problem
of low visibility, resulting in lower evaluations on the average for
women, creates the *stacked-deck effect. The stacked-deck effect refers
to the advantages that men have over women as the faculty commences
decision making about individual students.*

Before we start looking at examples of the stacked-deck effect, two
very important points need to be noted. First, if you sit down to play
a game of, say, blackjack, and the card deck is stacked against you,
this does *not* mean that you are guaranteed to lose on any particular
hand. Indeed, you may win several hands in a row. What it does
mean is that in the long run you are more likely to lose than to win.
How *much* more likely depends on how badly the deck is stacked.

The analogy goes like this: the existence of the stacked-deck effect
does not mean that all faculty decisions are disadvantageous to particular women. Individual women may ''win'' on any given occasion. What it does mean is that *on the average,* a man is more likely
to ''win'' than a woman with exactly the same qualifications. Just
how big this advantage is depends on how badly the deck is stacked.
This chapter will show how to even out the odds.

The second point that needs to be made about the stacked-deck
effect is that it applies to the conditions that obtain when the faculty
starts decision making—that is, given the setup at the beginning, all
other things being equal, men may have advantages over women.
To go back to our analogy, this means that if the deck is stacked
against you in a card game, the cards that are dealt to you initially
are less likely to be good than they would otherwise be. But once
the cards have been dealt, a lot depends on what you do with them.
Part of being a good card player is knowing how to play with bad
cards, so that in the long run you will still do well. The same point
applies here. *Part of being successful in winning the advantages that
faculty deal out is knowing how to play with the cards you've got.* Even

after the cards are dealt, there's a lot you can do to increase your chances of winning.

Grades and Evaluations by Individual Professors

The simplest case of faculty decision making is that in which an individual professor is making decisions about grades for students in a particular class. We already have a number of reasons to think that women could run into the stacked-deck effect at this level. Lower visibility of women and a tendency to rate women's work lower may lead a professor to give a lower grade to a woman than would be given to a comparable man. This will of course be particularly true in courses where grading is highly subjective, and not based on strictly numerical scores on exams or problem sets.

For example, consider Leslie's case:

Leslie is taking an urban studies course. There are about thirty students in the class. The final grade is based on the midterm and the final exam. Both exams have several multiple choice and true/false questions, and one or two essay questions. Leslie does well on both exams, and receives a B− for the course. In fact, if not for certain points subtracted from her essay questions, she would have received a B+. There are no comments on the exams to indicate precisely why the professor was not giving her full credit for these questions. It may be that there are good reasons. But Leslie very rarely speaks in class, and in the absence of any particular reason to assess her talents differently, the professor may simply "feel" that the essays are not quite up to B+ quality. Leslie is planning to take another course with this professor, and she realizes that she will have to work even harder to get an A than she would if she were more vocal in class or, perhaps, if she were a man.

On the average, women tend to be quieter in class than men, and this too makes the deck stacked. Therefore, a woman may have to work harder than a man to receive the same grade. Note that working harder is a way of compensating after the "cards" have been dealt. This is one way in which women have been evening out the odds for years.

It is possible for women to face disadvantages in courses where grading is based on strictly numerical measures as well. This happens, for example, in subjects for which women tend to have less preparation in high school than men. You didn't start learning the hidden curriculum only when you got to college!

The stacked-deck effect can work in just the same way when it comes to securing letters of recommendation to graduate or professional school. If you have tended to be less visible to your professors, and if your work has been underrated, then you will have a harder time finding professors to write outstanding letters on your behalf. Since outstanding letters of recommendation increase your chances of getting into the postgraduate programs of your choice, a deck stacked against women in this way may put them at a disadvantage in postgraduate applications relative to their male peers.

But whether or not a particular woman faces the stacked-deck effect in the awarding of grades in a particular class or in the receipt of a good letter of recommendation from a particular professor is entirely dependent on the individual class, the individual professor, and the individual student. There is no reason to assume that you face this problem in classes you are taking at the moment.

Faculty Decisions Made in Meetings

It is easy to see how the deck is stacked when it comes to decisions made at full faculty meetings as well. For instance, consider the way in which departmental Honors are awarded. Many colleges award Honors to graduating students with outstanding records. Honors are usually recorded on your transcript, and are one of the items that graduate or professional schools as well as employers may look for in considering your application.

Some departments may award Honors strictly on the basis of grade-point average in the field. In this case, assuming that women have not been subjected to the stacked-deck effect in the awarding of grades, they won't face the stacked-deck effect in the awarding of Honors. But in some departments the awarding of Honors is based on grade-point average plus the faculty's general evaluation of the talents and prospects of individual students. In this case, the decision as to who will receive Honors is generally made either by a committee of professors or at a full faculty meeting of the department.

Here's how the discussion at a faculty meeting might go.

Martha is a graduating senior majoring in communications arts, and she maintains a 3.75 grade-point average in that field. The full faculty of the Communications Arts department is meeting to decide which of its fifteen senior majors will be awarded Honors. The first thing they do is to decide that only those graduating seniors with departmental averages of 3.3 or above will be considered. This leaves them with six students. They would like to restrict the award to only three or four students, deemed truly outstanding. The faculty review the remaining six students one at a time, with various professors commenting on the student's overall performance in their classes, or any independent study work that the student has done for them. On the basis of this discussion, they compile their final list of students who seem the most promising. Martha is not on this list. This is not because anyone had anything to say that suggested that she shouldn't be—in fact, those professors who taught her remember Martha as a good student. They simply don't recall her as an outstanding student. No single professor has ever seen more than one or two papers of hers, and no one remembers either her written work or her class participation in any detail.

It is virtually impossible for decisions made in this way to be based solely on the academic merit of individual students, because *at the beginning of the decision-making process, the odds favor the more visible student, not necessarily the better student.* So while any particular woman may receive Honors in her major field, it is less likely as a rule that there will be at least one professor at the faculty meeting who knows her work well enough to recommend her for Honors than would be the case for one of her comparably qualified male peers.

Exactly the same sort of considerations applies to departmental decision making concerning the awarding of academic prizes. Many departments have certain prizes that they award each year to outstanding majors in the field. Sometimes these prizes involve a small stipend, but usually their principal advantage is prestige. Academic prizes are nice to list on your graduate or professional school applications, and on employment applications as well. If women face the stacked-deck effect in the awarding of academic prizes, they will face a disadvantage in postgraduate education and employment applications relative to their male peers.

Study-Related Jobs
Here's another example of the stacked-deck effect.

Nadia is currently attending Professor Navarro's seminar in sociology, Nadia's major field. Nadia is becoming very interested in the research that Professor Navarro (a man) is doing. She is an active participant in the seminar, and Professor Navarro gives every indication of thinking highly of her work. One day Nadia learns that Professor Navarro has hired another student in the seminar, Nick, to be a research assistant on his project. Nadia is very disappointed that Professor Navarro did not offer her the position, and she doesn't understand the decision. Nick is a mediocre student, who does not participate as actively as Nadia in the seminar, and who is majoring in a different field.

Of course, there may be extenuating circumstances of which Nadia is not aware. But in all probability what happened is quite simple: Professor Navarro simply did not consider Nadia for the position.

Low visibility was undoubtedly a factor here. While Nadia thought of herself as being a highly visible member of the seminar, Professor Navarro may not have been as aware of her participation in the class as he would have been were she a man. The fact that Professor Navarro hears Nadia each time she speaks in class, and thinks well of each of her papers, does not guarantee that he will conceive of her as making a valuable contribution to the seminar overall. Professor Navarro's perception of Nadia's contribution as a whole may be less than the sum of its parts.

But when it comes to the assignment of jobs, a further dimension is added to the problem of low visibility for women. The awarding of grades or other academic prizes involves professors' views of students *as students:* the evaluation involved pertains to the student's academic performance alone. Decisions concerning job appointments, however, involve an evaluation not only of the student's academic abilities but of the student's *job profile* as well.

A student's job profile consists of all those things aside from academic performance that make the student a promising or not-so-promising candidate for a job. In evaluating a student's job profile, a professor may consider her seriousness or dedication to the work. The professor may reason that the student who is more likely to pursue postgraduate work in the field has more need of undergraduate work experience in the field. Or, a job profile might include the professor's evaluation of how well the student is suited to the work. Even an academically well-qualified student might be viewed as not being well suited to certain sorts of work, depending on the professor's general conceptions of the work and the student. Another thing that a professor might take into consideration in making a job appointment could be whether the professor envisioned getting along well with the student under work conditions, and this too would become part of the job profile. Or again, a professor might consider financial need as part of the job profile, since the job involves a salary.

When Nadia was not offered the research position, it may well have been because Professor Navarro's assessment of her job profile was not that high, in spite of her academic achievements. Professor Navarro may have had a hard time thinking of Nadia as a dedicated student, likely to pursue postgraduate work in the field, or as someone well suited to the field. Such judgments concerning her job profile might have been heavily influenced by Professor Navarro's inability to think of women as serious scholars in his area, or as future professionals in the field. Or Professor Navarro might have assumed that Nadia was more likely to marry and stay home with children than to pursue a profession.

Furthermore, Professor Navarro may have a harder time envisioning a friendly working relationship with Nadia than with a man, since Professor Navarro may himself feel awkward or uncomfortable about working with a woman, or at any rate he may be more at ease working with men.

Finally, it is still common for people to assume that men need incomes in order to support themselves and possibly their families, while women are more likely to be thought of as being supported by someone else and therefore less in need of incomes of their own. But Nadia is supporting a child while putting herself through college, and any money she can earn through an educationally valuable position, such as the one Professor Navarro is offering, is that much more important.

In evaluating Nadia's job profile, Professor Navarro need not have engaged in any maliciousness or deliberate discrimination at all. In fact, what very likely happened is that Professor Navarro never even considered Nadia's job profile, since for all the reasons mentioned it may never have occurred to him to consider her for the position.

The problem of lower job-profile evaluations is also a problem of visibility. The deck may be stacked against Nadia at the outset, but if she can get Professor Navarro to *think* about her job profile, he may very well form a positive opinion. In order to beat the odds, Nadia needs some ways of increasing the visibility of her job profile.

Research assistantships are extremely valuable to the students who hold them. In addition to providing income, they provide valuable work and educational experience, important personal contact with a faculty member, and all the advantages for the course of the individual's future education and employment that come with that relationship and work. But such jobs are awarded almost entirely on the basis of an individual professor's assessment of the student. Hence the stacked-deck effect can produce a discriminatory impact on women by reducing their access to valuable educational and employment opportunities.

Research positions of the sort that Professor Navarro was able to offer are not extremely common at the undergraduate level. And, in order for a particular professor to be in a position to hire students, the professor generally needs a research grant of some sort. As a result, such positions are more likely to become available in the sciences than in the humanities. But even there, if the department has a graduate program, most of these jobs go to the graduate students. A more common form of employment opportunity comes in the form of teaching assistantships offered by departments.

Many departments will pay undergraduates to lead discussion or recitation sections for large classes, or to grade problem sets and exams. These positions offer income and sometimes valuable work experience, in addition to contributing to the overall impressiveness of a student's undergraduate record. Decisions about who gets these jobs are generally made at full faculty meetings, although individual professors may be given special influence when hiring teaching assistants for their own courses. By now it should be clear how the deck might be stacked here too.

Paternalism

If you have been turned down for a teaching assistantship that you were a candidate for, you will probably never know the reasons why. This kind of decision making is conducted almost entirely behind closed doors, and undergraduates are virtually never in on discussions at which such decisions are made. You may, however, be given a reason for the decision in your case.

The most frequent sort of explanation offered to women who have not been given an award or appointment is a paternalistic one. Paternalism involves a decision made for the good of another, which means in these cases for the student's own good. Here's an example of a paternalistic explanation.

Opal is a junior majoring in geology. The geology department has just decided which members of the junior class will be given teaching assistantships for the following year. Opal thinks that she has a pretty good chance of getting one. While she is not one of the top students in the program, there are many positions available, and most of her class will get one position or another. When the list of appointments is posted, however, her name is not on it. A few days after the decision was made, one of the male professors in the department, Professor O'Connors, with whom she has taken a couple of courses, tells her not to take the decision too much to heart. "It's not that the department didn't feel you were smart enough," Professor O'Connors tells her, "it's just that we thought that since you already spend so much time at basketball practice, you probably wouldn't want to spend a lot of time grading papers too."

If the reason Professor O'Connors gives Opal for the department's decision is in fact the one that the department based its decision on, then the department has made a decision on paternalistic grounds. The basis for the decision has been that Opal would be better off, or perhaps happier, without the additional work load of a teaching assistantship. Note that Professor O'Connors does not explain to Opal, for instance, that the department felt that her academic record was not strong enough to indicate that she could handle the teaching assistantship in addition to basketball practice. Rather, the explanation offered is that she would not *want* the additional work.

Whether or not Opal wants the teaching assistantship is something that Opal could decide for herself. If the department had offered it to her and she had felt that she was already too busy to take on additional responsibilities, then she could have declined it. *A paternalistic decision is one made on behalf of the student, as if the student were not capable of making a reasonable decision on her own.*

There is no way to ascertain in the abstract whether a paternalistic decision of this sort involves any kind of discrimination. The question is whether the department would have taken a male student's sports activities into consideration in the same way. Since people tend to think in different ways about women and men, it is frequently the case that different considerations enter into decision making when women are being discussed than when men are being discussed. Hence it is possible that the department would not have considered a male student's athletic activities in the same light as Opal's.

However, the only evidence Opal could have would be if she knew of a male student who was on a school team and who had been given a teaching assistantship. And even in this case, before Opal could be sure that she had been discriminated against on the basis of gender, she would probably need to know that the male student's academic record was comparable to hers, and perhaps need to know of other cases of men on teams who were given assistantships and women on teams who were denied them. It is not likely that Opal will be able to discern this sort of pattern.

Furthermore, Opal has no way of knowing whether the explanation she was given for not getting an assistantship was in fact the reason that the department as a whole based its decision on. The department's decision might have been made without any discussion of Opal's being on the basketball team at all. In reporting the basis for the decision to Opal, Professor O'Connors might have been expressing an interpretation of the departmental discussion that others on the faculty would not agree with, or Professor O'Connors might simply have been making something up in order to make Opal feel better about not getting the job.

This brings us to the heart of the problem with paternalistic explanations. The mere fact that Professor O'Connors *explained* the department's decision to Opal in a paternalistic manner is a problem in and of itself, quite independently of whether or not the decision itself was made on paternalistic grounds. The explanation conveys two clear messages to Opal.

The first message is that Professor O'Connors feels that Opal will "take it too much to heart" if she believes that the decision was based on academic merit. The implication is that Professor O'Connors does not expect Opal to be able to handle criticism or failure. The professor's remark communicates to Opal the professor's expectations of her, and these expectations affect Opal's experience of the situation.

The sort of "consolation" that Opal was offered is very seldom given to male students. Professors tend to expect men to handle failure in a constructive way, and they communicate this expectation in explaining decisions to male students. Over a period of time, women and men learn two different sorts of lessons about their own capacities to withstand failure. In fact, women do tend to take academic failure or rejection "more to heart" than their male peers, presuming that failure is a direct reflection of their own incompetence and lack of worth, while men might assume some incompetence or error in judgment on the parts of those making the decisions.

While Professor O'Connors's paternalistic explanation may sincerely be intended to keep Opal from feeling bad, in fact it teaches her to feel *worse* about the decision than if she had been given no explanation at all. The very fact that a paternalistic explanation is offered to her indicates that in the professor's opinion, Opal needs to be protected from the implications of her failure to get an assistantship. In fact, this offer of protection reinforces Opal's inclination to view the department's decision as something she ought to be taking very much to heart.

The second message carried by the explanation offered to Opal is closely related to the first: it suggests to Opal that the department didn't think that Opal would be capable of knowing what was best for her and deciding for herself. This is the essence of all paternalistic explanations. Professor O'Connors's remark, no matter how well motivated, suggests that the department is choosing to treat Opal as a child. As Opal is constantly treated like a child in the course of her college education, she may come to feel increasingly like a child.

Since women and men enter college already having been socialized differently in many respects, they are likely to respond differently to paternalistic remarks. While a male student being given a paternalistic explanation may immediately recognize that his own decision making has been superseded, a woman, accustomed to being treated as a child in certain ways, may not notice the peculiarity of the remark at all. In this way, paternalistic remarks can contribute in different ways to the socialization of women and men even when they are made to both women and men. However, if you start counting the number of paternalistic explanations offered to women compared with the number offered to men, you will find that faculty are far more likely to "console" women in this way. Paternalistic remarks are one way in which professors, often wholly without awareness of what they are doing, socialize women to be more childlike in their relationships to others in the college community than men are.

While paternalistic explanations may tend to teach women to feel crushed by failure, and to accept routinely the tendency of others to make decisions on their behalf as if they were incapable of reasonable decision making on their own, they can serve this function only so long as women listen to them uncritically. Just as with many of the problems discussed in Get Smart Courses 101 and 202, the key to beating the problem of paternalistic remarks is to learn to hear them differently.

Before leaving the subject of paternalism, it is worth making a further remark or two on the motivations behind paternalistic decision making. Professors are in an almost parental role with respect to their students. They are teachers, sometimes mentors; they are responsible for the assignment of rewards for good work and criticism for bad; and they may play a large role in guiding the student toward certain choices for postgraduate life, and in determining the extent to which these choices are attainable. So, to many people, it seems natural and appropriate that professors make decisions based not only on the academic quality of a student's written work or classroom participation but on what the faculty judges to be in the general interest of the student as well.

But in point of fact, if you fill a room with a group of people who have certain ideas about the general tendencies, traits, and talents of women versus those of men, and if you ask the people in this room to make decisions for the good of the individuals under consideration, the decisions will almost inevitably reflect the preconceptions and prejudices of the deciding parties. No matter how well intentioned the decision making may be, the acceptance of paternalistic reasoning leads to the stacked-deck effect in academic decision making concerning individual women. It is important not to be misled by paternalism. *Paternalistic behavior always appears well intentioned. But beware: intentions are irrelevant. Paternalism is no excuse for discrimination!*

One of the reasons that paternalistic thinking on the part of faculty can be dangerous is that it allows people to employ their preconceptions and stereotypes uncritically when making decisions. A sort of paternalism may also underlie the tendency of people in positions of authority, for example, advisers or professors, systematically to encourage women to enter certain areas of study or to avoid others, while systematically counseling men in different ways. Such a practice can be motivated by prejudice or by pure habit on the part of the adviser. But it can also be in large measure motivated by the feeling the adviser may have that certain students will be happier or better off in certain areas of study. This may be what happened in Peggy's case:

Peggy is a sophomore in the process of choosing a major. She goes to see her assigned guidance counselor to discuss the matter. While she hasn't made up her mind completely, she is leaning toward a major in metallurgy when the conversation begins. But the guidance counselor strongly urges Peggy to reconsider, giving several reasons: first, the counselor talks about the difficulty of getting fellowship money for graduate study in that area, and since Peggy will certainly need financial support in order to continue studying, this is of major concern; second, the counselor tells Peggy that the field is extremely competitive, and this scares Peggy a bit; and third, she is told that this is a field that does not offer lucrative employment possibilities, which is something that Peggy thought it did. The guidance counselor is clearly convinced that Peggy would be happier in some other field, and some of this conviction begins to dampen Peggy's enthusiasm for metallurgy.

In this case, the adviser may be sincerely attempting to keep the student from making a decision that will result in the student's unhappiness. This is, after all, to a large extent what an adviser is supposed to do. But it may also be that the adviser is in no real position to know anything about fellowships or employment prospects or the student's ability to excel in that field. In this way, advisers and professors can inadvertently limit the options that both women and men have, by allowing their advice to be influenced by their own preconceptions and prejudices about what is good for the student.

Stereotyping and Discrimination

Stereotyping can lead to other forms of the stacked-deck effect for women, as well as to outright sex discrimination. Let's consider what happened to Quintana. Quintana qualifies for her college's work-study program, a federally run program that subsidizes on-campus and some off-campus employment for students demonstrating financial need. Both the establishment of financial need and the awarding of the right to a work-study job are areas of decision making that are subject to control of the governing federal agencies. In addition, work-study wage levels are fixed by federal guidelines. Thus, women should not face sex discrimination in securing work-study positions. Nevertheless, they may still face the stacked-deck effect. Here's how it works in Quintana's case.

Quintana has filed an application for a work-study position with the appropriate office on her campus, and her application has been approved. This means that she has demonstrated the level of financial need required for eligibility to the work-study program. She then goes to the on-campus employment service and inquires about work-study positions currently available. She is told that there is not much available at the moment, but that there is one very attractive opening in the office of the department of comparative literature. Quintana goes to the comparative literature department office, meets with the administrative assistant there, and within a few days begins working fifteen hours a week in the office. Her job involves filing, a small amount of typing, and answering the phone. The job title is Clerical Assistant, and, in accordance with the federal guidelines for salaries for positions with this title, she is paid minimum wage. A few weeks after she begins work, she learns of a male student who had been to the employment office during the same week she was looking for a job, and who had been offered a position as a research assistant in the classics department at a higher salary than hers. The position he obtained did not require any special expertise or experience, nor any particular field of study.

Quintana's case illustrates several aspects of the stacked-deck effect, as well as certain elements of sex discrimination in the strict sense.

The stacked-deck effect may be working against Quintana as soon as she reports to the on-campus employment office. While the federal government regulates eligibility for work-study positions, neither the government nor the college administration has direct control over which job goes to which student. People who work in employment offices may, like the advisers we discussed a moment ago, steer different students toward different positions out of some sense of which jobs would be "right" for the students. The person who referred Quintana to the secretarial position may have thought that Quintana would not like the research job, and for this reason simply have failed to mention it to her.

This problem can also crop up when the student does not go through a campus employment office. Various offices and agencies within the university are allotted funds to hire a certain number of work-study students. As positions become available, these offices will generally advertise them on local bulletin boards. It is up to the person in charge of hiring for that position to decide which students to hire. Feelings that people may have about the inappropriateness of secretarial work for men, or the appropriateness of secretarial work for women, may lead them to prefer female candidates for secretarial work and male candidates for research work.

The practice of refusing to hire women for certain kinds of work on campus is, of course, discriminatory and illegal. But people's feelings and tendencies often enter the picture in ways that make the charge of discrimination hard to substantiate. If you feel that you have been denied a job on the basis of gender, you should read Get Smart Course 404 on substantiating and correcting sex discrimination on campus.

Word-of-Mouth Job Advertising
Aside from the issue of sex discrimination in the hiring decision itself, the problem is exacerbated by the fact that many on-campus jobs are advertised by word of mouth. When a department or pro-

fessor is looking for a research assistant, members of the faculty may approach certain students, explaining the job and encouraging them to apply for it or to pass the word on to friends. The stacked-deck effect enters the picture here in exactly the same way as in other faculty decisions. Because women tend to have lower visibility than their male peers, and because their job profiles may be evaluated differently, they may be less likely to be approached when desirable positions become available. In this way, even a department that might very well have hired a woman had she applied may never have the opportunity, since qualified women may have a hard time finding out about such positions before they have been filled.

Notice that the situation may be different when a department is looking for a secretarial worker. Individual professors seldom get involved in recruiting for such positions, with the result that applicants are more likely to know about the position from the employment office or from a job advertisement. Since male work-study students may have an easier time finding jobs without going through an office or advertisement, more of the candidates applying for the secretarial positions may indeed be women. Not all problems of inequity in hiring decisions can be reduced to cases of people preferring men to women for certain sorts of work and women to men for others. The stacked-deck effect can influence patterns of hiring distribution on campus in various and subtle ways. That is one reason why it is so important to learn to overcome it.

What Makes One Job Better Than Another?

There are good reasons why the research assistantship that the male student got may be a more desirable position than the one Quintana got. A research assistant has the opportunity to develop a close working relationship with a professor, an important path to high visibility. The professor is then in a position to assist the student in securing various advantages, such as prizes or entrance to graduate school, by writing letters of recommendation and by recommending the student for Honors and other research projects.

The professor can provide individual attention and encouragement to the student, even in cases where the student's major field of study lies outside the domain of the research. In addition, the research job can provide a valuable educational experience, one that can be helpful in securing further work and educational opportunities, since it looks very good on a resume. In all of these ways, the research position can provide rich educational opportunities, important high visibility connections, and the opportunity to enter into the intellectual life of the college in a new way, gaining the attention of the faculty in the process.

The secretarial position, on the other hand, does not provide the opportunity for the student to forge academic relations with members of the faculty. Such work will seldom contribute to the student's preparation for graduate or professional school, or for any line of postgraduation work other than secretarial. In addition, by holding a secretarial position, the female student is even less apt than otherwise to be perceived by faculty members of that department as a serious member of the academic community.

Thus simple biases and habits of thought and small differences in patterns of employment for women and men can lead to a situation in which the deck is stacked against women. And even small things can have far-reaching educational consequences for the woman affected.

Salary and Job Descriptions

There is one aspect of Quintana's situation that we have not yet touched on: salary. Depending on Quintana's circumstances, salary may be the single most important aspect of whatever employment she is able to find on campus. While the law requires equal pay for work-study jobs with equal job descriptions or titles, it does not entirely determine which job will be given which title, or which student will be hired at which level. The job Quintana is referred to receives lower salary than the job the male student is referred to because the job description suggests less experience required or less responsibility held. In fact, the experience required for the research job was in this case no greater than the experience required for the secretarial job. Insofar as Quintana was steered to a secretarial position because she is a woman, she has been discriminated against.

Job descriptions, which in turn determine salary, are often set by the person who is the student's immediate supervisor. Within limits, the stacked-deck effect can surface here, too, to create one form of sex discrimination. Since a supervisor may be inclined to view work performed by a woman as less important or requiring less skill than work performed by a man, it may sometimes happen that two work-study students sharing equivalent job responsibilities may work under different job titles, hence at different salaries. In an office with a complex and ill-defined set of daily tasks, for instance, it would be quite easy for a woman to be hired under the job title of Clerk Typist at \$4.05 per hour, while a man with overlapping and equivalent responsibilities is called an Office Assistant and receives \$4.50 per hour. Or, it may happen that after some period of time a man is promoted to such a title and salary raise, while it simply does not occur to the supervisor to promote the woman.

A related problem is that people tend to evaluate the job profiles of women differently than the job profiles of men in ways we have already discussed, and a professor or department might make a request of you for some labor entirely without pay. While it may be appropriate in some cases, there is a tendency for professors to find it reasonable to request research assistance from women or to request that women students assist with secretarial tasks or, for instance, in organizing and running departmental social functions, without any monetary compensation.

It is often not clear that one is better off turning down such a request than honoring it, and it is seldom easy to ascertain in any particular case whether a man would have been offered money for the work. But in instances in which professors wish to request such volunteer work from students, they are more likely to turn to female than to male students.

Sex Discrimination Compounded by Other Forms of Discrimination

It is important to note that certain groups of women will encounter sex discrimination with greater regularity than other groups. For instance, if Leslie is black, then she may have an even harder time getting the professor to overcome that ill-defined feeling that her essays aren't quite up to B+ quality. If the professors of the communications arts department have seen Martha around the department with her child, and think of her primarily as a mother, then they may be that much less inclined to single her out for the kind of award that signals promise in a professional field.

Suppose Nadia speaks English as a second language, but not completely fluently. Even though Professor Navarro thinks well of her work, he may be even more inclined to underrate it when it comes time for an overall evaluation. It is often difficult for people fully to appreciate intelligence when it is expressed in faltering language, and Professor Navarro may be even less inclined to consider her as a prospective research assistant.

If Opal is a lesbian and members of the faculty are even vaguely aware of this, then she may simply be disliked or distrusted, and the faculty may be averse to giving her a teaching assistantship that would bring her into working relationships with them.

If Peggy goes to meet her guidance counselor in a wheelchair, then the counselor may be that much less inclined to view metallurgy as an appropriate major for Peggy, without having any real idea of what the field involves or of what Peggy's talents are.

If Quintana is a Native American, then getting herself recommended for a research position in the classics department over a secretarial position in the comparative literature department may be that much more difficult.

The same features of prejudice and stereotyping that can contribute to the stacked-deck effect for all women can be compounded by these additional factors. In all of these cases, low expectations can become self-fulfilling in that the fewer opportunities and advantages a student is given, the more restrictive her educational experiences are, and thus the fewer her future options may become.

Many of the problems we have discussed in this section can be serious if they go by unchecked, since they have a certain discriminatory impact on women. At the same time, most of these problems can be remedied to a greater or lesser extent, as discussed in the "Solutions" section.

Solutions

The "Problems" section of this chapter illustrated an array of problems, ranging from minor instances of the stacked-deck effect to discriminatory pay practices that the stacked-deck effect can produce. The stacked-deck effect is in large measure an outgrowth of the problems discussed in Get Smart Courses 101 and 202. The relatively low visibility of women in the classroom and the difficulties in forming close working relationships with individual professors have far-reaching implications. They have a discriminatory impact on women in matters concerning the distribution by faculty of valuable awards and opportunities.

This is a good time to go back and review the "Solutions" sections of Get Smart Courses 101 and 202. The problems outlined in this chapter should make even clearer the value of cultivating high visibility and creating a counter-curriculum in the college classroom. Learning to be a more assertive participant in classroom discussion not only enhances your self-esteem, it helps you counteract the stacked-deck effect by increasing your visibility.

Since the problem of low visibility for women in the classroom has to do not only with the tendency of individual women to be quiet and deferential but also with the general tendency of professors to rate the work of women lower than men's, it is important to change the lessons taught by the hidden curriculum concerning the differences between women and men generally. Only after the counter-curriculum is installed in the classroom can you be sure that your work will be given the full credit it deserves.

Gaining visibility in the classroom involves both learning to be more active in class and learning to help teach the counter-curriculum in your classes. If you review the "Solutions" section of Get Smart Course 101 now, you may be surprised at how little you will need to do in order to make large gains in visibility for yourself and the other women in your classes.

Get Smart Course 202 is useful in this respect, too. Students who do not have any close working relationships with individual professors are at a disadvantage when the faculty makes decisions concerning a large number of matters. This may be particularly important in schools or departments that offer large lecture classes, where professors have virtually no other way of getting to know the work of individual students. But even in small classes (unless you attend a women's college) academic visibility with individual professors will be more of a problem for women than for men. Therefore, it is important that you not be hindered in your efforts to work with professors outside the classroom.

If you review the "Solutions" section of Get Smart Course 202, you will find that there are relatively simple steps you can take in order to overcome many of the difficulties of working with professors. These steps lead to a lessening of the stacked-deck effect as well. Get Smart Course 202 can help even out the odds.

The lessons of Get Smart Course 101 can also be applied to undoing the stacked-deck effect when it comes to grading or asking professors for letters of recommendation. It is extremely rare for a professor intentionally to give a low grade to a student because she is a woman, or for a professor to be aware of grading women's work by a different standard than men's. When the stacked-deck effect does occur in grading, it is generally because the professor unwittingly perceives work done by women differently than work done by men, or because the professor allows high visibility in class to be a factor in grading. In the latter case, the professor may not be aware that high visibility is a factor. But even where this criterion is made explicit, the professor is not likely to conceive of it as a practice with a discriminatory impact on women.

That is to say, the stacked-deck effect is most likely to crop up in classes where women themselves have the hardest time gaining the kind of classroom visibility that would even out the odds. They are often the classes in which the hidden curriculum is most consistently taught. The degree to which the hidden curriculum is taught in a class indicates the degree to which the professor accepts its lessons—

probably wholly unwittingly—and, as a result, the extent of the difficulties that women may have in excelling in the class. Therefore, the degree to which the hidden curriculum is taught in your classes is one of the best indicators you can have of the likelihood of the stacked-deck effect playing a role in those classes.

As you and your friends start watching out for the hidden curriculum, you can trade observations on different classes. In this way you gain information about large numbers of classes, which can help you in planning your course schedule. Naturally, you should not avoid taking classes that are important to you simply because the hidden curriculum is taught in them—that would be cutting off your nose to spite your face. And besides, by now you are equipped not only to overcome the old hidden curriculum but to begin teaching the counter-curriculum as well.

But you might want to steer yourself toward courses in which the hidden curriculum is minimal. For instance, you might have a choice between different sections of the same course, or between two or three courses that are in some ways equally important or interesting to you. In such cases, information about the hidden curriculum taught in those classes can help you find more rewarding, less aggravating classes. In addition, you might want to avoid professors who are particularly difficult on this subject, if possible.

But the important rule to remember is that if you want to reduce the extent to which the deck may be stacked against you as much as possible, then you must make the most strenuous effort to do so in classes where the hidden curriculum is most adamantly taught. These will be the classes in which the stacked-deck effect is most likely to occur. If you wish to even out the odds, then it is important to employ the techniques discussed in Get Smart Course 101 for gaining visibility and teaching the counter-curriculum in those classes where the hidden curriculum is most obvious.

Working on Your Job Profile
Anything you do to gain visibility in the classroom and in working relationships with individual professors will reduce the stacked-deck effect when it comes to the awarding of Honors and academic prizes as well. It will also help when it comes to the selection of students for jobs, such as the one that Nadia did not get as a research assistant to a professor she was working with.

One of Nadia's problems was probably low visibility. But this low visibility was not the result of Nadia's being a quiet or reserved student, or the result of the professor's low evaluation of any of the papers she wrote for him. In Nadia's case, it seems that the professor may have considered the whole—Nadia's total contribution to the seminar and her potential in the field—as being less than the sum of the parts—each of Nadia's individual contributions in the form of classroom participation and papers. This is probably a simple result of the professor's habits of thought. Is there anything Nadia can do to increase her visibility?

There certainly is. Remember that Nadia's visibility problem probably became an issue at the point when her job profile became relevant. It is not the case that the professor did not recognize the quality of her work. What happened is that when the professor needed to hire someone, Nadia was probably not considered as a possible research assistant. Nadia's problem isn't a low academic evaluation, but a low job profile evaluation. That is something she can fix.

We pointed out in the "Problems" section that in all probability, Professor Navarro simply did not consider Nadia because of the low visibility of her job profile. It is quite likely that had he stopped to consider her job profile, the matter might have turned out differently. But even in this case, it is quite possible that Professor Navarro would have made certain assumptions about Nadia's job profile that would have been both unwarranted and detrimental to his overall evaluation. For instance, if Professor Navarro is in the habit of assuming that women are in general not dedicated to the profession in this field, then he might tend to assume that Nadia is not in need of research experience as much as a man might be.

What Professor Navarro lacks is information about Nadia. In the absence of this information, he is likely to follow his assumptions uncritically, because *he has no cause to reconsider them.* All that Nadia has to do in order to remedy this situation is to give him cause to reconsider. She has to give him information.

Here's what Nadia should do. She should sit down and write out a list of all the reasons she wants a research assistantship with Professor Navarro. Then she should add to the list all the qualifications she has for the work and all those aspects of her education and plans that make her well suited for it. She should include her academic qualifications, such as her grades in Professor Navarro's class and other classes in related areas; the degree to which she is interested in pursuing postgraduate work in the field; those aspects of her personality that make her well suited to work in the field. She might list, for instance, her aptitude for a certain kind of thinking, her patience with a certain kind of experimental setup, or anything else that might be relevant to the work in question.

There are two things that Nadia can do with this list. One is to prepare a short statement on the basis of it, which she can then recite to Professor Navarro. This statement should be brief, but it should include all the items Nadia considers to be selling points in her favor. She can then approach Professor Navarro after class, during office hours, or by appointment, and provide him with the information she has assembled regarding her job profile. She might start off by saying something like this:

> I've heard that you might be looking for a research assistant. I am very interested in working for you, and I also think I would be good at it. I'm doing very well in my sociology classes: my grades are all B+ or better, and I am an active participant in all of my classes. I am seriously considering going to graduate school in this field, because I think that this sort of work is very interesting and also something that I do well. I'm good with statistical analysis, and I have a great deal of patience for long, involved processes of data collection. I'm also careful and meticulous in my work.
>
> I think you would find that I would be a diligent and useful assistant, and I know that the work experience would be good preparation for graduate school.

You might think that you would be too uncomfortable selling yourself this way. Never mind that. The fact is that if Nadia doesn't do a little selling, Professor Navarro will lack enough information to raise her job profile evaluation and Nadia will have missed out on a rich educational opportunity. A little discomfort is a small price to pay for the kind of experience that Nadia might have if she gets the position. You can probably see this point in Nadia's case, but you may find it harder to convince yourself in your own case.

Sit down in peace and quiet for five minutes and consider how badly you want the research position. Think of all that it offers you and what possibilities it may open up for the future. Then ask yourself if all of that is worth five minutes of slight discomfort. It undoubtedly is. You might be surprised to learn that your male peers do this sort of thing all the time. It is not an unheard-of practice for students to try to convince professors of their talents and ambitions. *In a game in which the deck is stacked against you to begin with, you can't afford to play your cards too conservatively. One bold move and you can swing the odds, not only so they're even but all the way around to your favor!*

If you still aren't convinced, or you really don't think you could go through with a conversation like this, then here's another suggestion. Try writing a brief summary of your qualifications and simply handing it over to the professor. This summary should include all the essentials, just as Nadia's monologue did, and it should be presented in a format that is easy to skim. It can be in the format of a letter or a resume. You might want to look at some sample resumes to see how this can be done. Your college placement office probably has some samples for you to study, and in addition may very well have a brochure on resume writing. Someone in the office might be able to help you prepare a good written statement.

A written statement that you prepare for a professor for whom you would like to work need not be in the form of a finished or completed resume. Much of what goes on a resume may be omissible. On the other hand, a professional-looking resume may be just what is called for. You might prepare a resume that stresses those aspects of your qualifications that are relevant to the research you are interested in, and then hand it over to the professor, saying something like this:

> I understand that you may be looking for an assistant. I am very interested in the position. I have prepared a resume to give you, so that you can see my qualifications for the work. I hope that you will give my interest in the work due consideration.

Your letter or resume should not be longer than one page, so that it can be quickly read. Then the professor need only spend a minute or two looking it over, and already your job profile may be evaluated in a completely new light.

By the way, it may be the case in many of your classes that the professor does not read papers or assign grades. Particularly in large classes, or classes with large amounts of problem sets or other written assignments, most of the grading may be done by upper-level undergraduate or graduate teaching assistants. In such a case, the professor may have no idea of what written work or which set of grades goes with which student in the class. Calling a professor's attention to your grades in that professor's class in not necessarily redundant.

What about Unannounced Job Openings?

You may have noticed that there is a part of Nadia's problem that we have completely overlooked until now. Nadia did not learn that there was a research position available until after it had been filled. Again, the problem is largely one of low visibility and low job profile evaluation, and the solution is to provide faculty with information of the sort that Nadia could have given Professor Navarro.

You should get into the habit of providing your professors with the information they will need in order to give you due consideration for any jobs that may come up. Prepare a resume, and update it from time to time. Then whenever you take a class with a professor whose work interests you, you can give the professor a copy of your resume, explaining that should the professor learn of any research positions that become available, you would be very interested in working as a research assistant in that field. Then, if the professor does hear of anything, or if the professor is at some point about to hire someone, the professor will more likely think of you as a candidate for the job, and can review your qualifications at a glance.

By advertising your interests and talents in this way as you go through college, you can virtually eliminate the stacked-deck effect in many areas of your experience. You gain visibility in this way that not only puts you in a good position to hear about and secure interesting work when it arises but also lets your professors know that you are a serious and ambitious student, one who deserves consideration for the various advantages that professors can offer their students.

When you reach the point at which you have declared your major, you might want to make an appointment with the Chair of your major department for the same purpose. You might briefly explain your interest in any research employment opportunities, or any postgraduate opportunities in the field that might arise. You could hand over a copy of your resume to the Chair. In this way, you are assured that your name will not simply be overlooked when research positions and other opportunities arise.

This is also a useful technique for securing teaching assistantships. If you let the Chair of the department know that you are interested in a teaching assistantship, and if you provide her with your qualifications, then your chances of getting an appointment are greatly increased. Once again, this may seem awkward or pushy to you, but you might be surprised at how often men will proclaim their interest in such a position loudly and clearly to professors in the department. The practice is not obnoxious; it is a perfectly reasonable way to see to it that professors have all the information they need when making decisions concerning you. And it is effective.

There is a further, and very important, side benefit of telling people what your interests and qualifications are: it short-circuits paternalistic thinking. A professor may reason that you would be better off without a certain research position, since it would require work that you would find too strenuous or unpleasant. This is paternalistic reasoning. If you *tell* the professor that you would enjoy the work and find it a welcome challenge, then the professor cannot employ the paternalistic argument. Similarly, a department may decide that a certain teaching assistantship would not be good for you, because the increased work load would be something you would not want. If you *tell* the Chair of the department, or someone else on the faculty of that department, that you would welcome and enjoy additional work, then this argument cannot be further employed.

The department may still decide not to give you the teaching assistantship. Nothing you do can guarantee that you will get what you want. But providing the department with the relevant information can ensure that when the department meets to make its decision, the odds in your case will be as favorable as they can be. Since paternalism may enter into decisions in such a way as to stack the deck against women, anything you can do to make paternalistic reasoning difficult will help even out the odds. *Paternalism works primarily by allowing people to reason in habitual ways in the absence of corrective information. Providing information about yourself to the faculty may be the single best tool you have against the negative effects of paternalism.*

Resisting Paternalism

Supplying faculty with information is a very effective way to prevent paternalistic behavior. Correction after the fact is a somewhat trickier matter. While paternalism may enter faculty decision making in a way that has discriminatory impact on women, establishing that this is the case in a particular department can be extremely difficult. To see why this is so, let's return to Opal's case.

Opal had been told by Professor O'Connors that the department had turned her down for a teaching assistantship on grounds that were paternalistic: they thought it would be too heavy a schedule for Opal to be on the basketball team and serve as a teaching assistant. A professor's report of departmental reasoning is probably the closest to direct evidence that the undergraduate will ever come. But as pointed out in the "Problems" section, this professor's remark is not proof of discriminatory practice.

In the first place, Opal has no way of knowing what the faculty really discussed at the meeting. Professor O'Connors may be mistaken about the faculty's reasons, or he may even be lying about them. And in the second place, Opal has no way of knowing whether the same reasoning has ever been, or ever would be, used in consideration of a man for an assistantship.

One of the complications here stems from what is meant by "the same reasoning." It is highly unlikely that a man who is on the basketball team is being considered for a position at the same time Opal is. In fact, it is probable that the department has not had a male major under consideration for a teaching assistantship in recent years who has been on the school basketball team. Therefore, if by "the same reasoning" we require that exactly the same argument was put forward in the consideration of a man for a position, Opal will never be able to demonstrate a discriminatory angle to the department's decision.

The way paternalism works, it may seldom turn out that exactly the same considerations are introduced in evaluating two students, one male and one female, where the male student receives the position in spite of or because of that consideration and the female is turned down because of it. Paternalism may work by shifting the emphasis in subtle ways that faculty place upon personality, outside activities, or social relationships in the job profiles of women and men. This can make paternalism an effective, but highly elusive, agent of discrimination. Get Smart Course 404 will discuss at greater length what you can do about discriminatory uses of paternalism.

Since the discrimination inherent in certain forms of paternalism is very hard to demonstrate in particular cases, the general preventive measure discussed above is that much more important. But you also need to be prepared to deal with paternalistic remarks when they occur. The paternalistic remark that Professor O'Connors made to Opal in explaining the department's decision had an immediate effect on her. The effects of such remarks are easy to gain control of, however, if you know how.

First, learn to recognize when a remark made to you by a professor is paternalistic. Is the professor suggesting something for your own good? Is the professor reporting that a decision was made for your own good, or that some decision should or will be made for your own good? Is the matter at hand something you could decide for yourself? *Whenever your decision making is circumvented or appropriated by a professor, adviser, administrator, or department "for your own good," you are being subjected to paternalism.*

As long as you can spot a paternalistic remark, you will have little trouble resisting its messages. Remember that Opal received two messages from Professor O'Connors's remarks. The first was that she was expected to take to heart her failure to get an assistantship. The second was that she was not mature enough to be permitted to decide for herself what was in her own best interests. As soon as Opal realizes that the professor's remarks are conveying these two messages, she can simply reject them.

Opal should bear in mind that the paternalistic remark is part of a pattern of socialization that teaches women to treat academic failure or rejection as a reflection or outcome of their own incompetence or unworthiness. And, indeed, women learn this lesson. Women, more than men, are inclined to assume that a professor's criticism reflects genuine flaws in their work. They are more likely than men to interpret a low grade on a paper as indicating their own stupidity or ineptness. They are more likely than men to interpret failure to receive a teaching assistantship as a reflection of their incompetence.

While it is a virtue to be appropriately humble, and while the criticisms that your professors offer of your work can be extremely valuable teaching tools, it is a mistake to presume that a professor's judgment or a department's decision necessarily reflects something about you or your work. How often have you heard a male student comment that a professor's grading or criticisms of his paper were simply misguided and mistaken? It may be that the paper was poor, and the criticisms just. But it is just as possible that the paper was good, and that the professor failed to give it due consideration or credit. Professors are only human. They have bad days, off semesters, and personal idiosyncrasies that can influence their judgments about students. In addition, if you stop to think about it you will realize that some of them value the same things in students' work that you do, but others simply do not.

Ironically, men often have an easier time distancing themselves from criticism and failure than women do, but women in the college community may have greater need to place things in perspective. Since the stacked-deck effect works against you in many areas, it is even more likely that a professor's criticism, or a department's decision, tells you extremely little about your own true talents or worthiness. More likely, it tells you something about the often irrational and biased ways in which human beings—professors included—sometimes make decisions.

The University Is Not a Meritocracy
You may hear that the university is a meritocracy: that the best and the brightest eventually rise to the top, and the mediocre and talentless sink to the bottom. Many people seem to think that the university ought to be a meritocracy, and hope that by believing strongly enough in the system they can help make it work as a meritocracy. But whether or not the university should be a meritocracy, the fact is that *no university in the country is a genuine meritocracy*. Who succeeds and who fails, who rises to the top and who sinks to the bottom, who accrues the honors and advantages that the university has to offer—all of this is determined by a complex web of social and

political factors, many of which have little to do with the relative merits of individuals.

In a sense, everything discussed in this book pertains to exactly this point. The entire book is about difficulties that women face in becoming those who "rise to the top" in the university, or those who excel by the university's own standards. *None* of the problems that impede women's success in college are a result of a lack of talent, intelligence, or academic potential on their part. Women face certain problems on the university campus that have nothing to do with merit or the absence of merit. *One of the most important lessons you can learn is that academic criticism, failure, or rejection does not necessarily have any more to do with your own talents and potential than, say, losing the lottery or, perhaps, losing a hand of poker. The reasons for your failure may have very little to do with you personally. And the skills required for success, such as those that gain high visibility, may have little to do with intelligence or academic talent.*

Counteracting Paternalistic Thinking
The only thing that academic failure, criticism, or rejection can be assumed to entail is the failure to secure some educational advantage that you might have wanted. Opal needs to learn how to get teaching assistantships. She needs to learn *not* to assume that she didn't get the job because she didn't deserve it. In her situation, reinforced by Professor O'Connors's "protective" remark, she may tend to assume that not getting the assistantship reflects her own stupidity or incompetence, even while she recognizes that some of the students who did get the appointments are not smarter or better students than she is.

Opal might be very quick to recognize when another student, perhaps a friend, is being treated like a child. At the same time, in her own case, the professor's explanation of how the department made its decision about her assistantship may not strike her as odd. Her tendency may be to accept the view that others know better than she does what will be good for her. It is possible, of course, that the professor or the department was right: maybe Opal would have accepted the assistantship, thinking she could handle the additional work, and then found that it was really too much for her. This eventuality is irrelevant. Opal must learn to reclaim responsibility for her own decision making and to take her own risks.

One thing Opal might want to do is to try putting herself in the professor's shoes. Suppose that Opal were a professor, and she was deciding whether to give a teaching assistantship to a student. Suppose she knew that the student was on the basketball team and spent a lot of time at practice. Just to stack the deck a little more, let's try to picture the student as a man. What would Opal do?

Our bet is that Opal would decide to ask the student whether he would have enough time for the job! Opal might advise the student that it might be unwise to take on so much additional work, but she would not be comfortable simply telling the student, "You won't be happy with so much work, so I'm not giving you the job." This would be to treat the student like a child, and to presume to know more about the student's time schedule and needs than he does. No matter how inadvisable Opal might think the combination of basketball and assistantship might be, she would not find it acceptable to explain her decision to the student in a paternalistic way. Opal should find Professor O'Connors's way of explaining the decision equally unacceptable.

What Opal Should Do

There are two things Opal can do at the time a paternalistic remark is made to her by a professor in order to take control immediately of the remark's effects. The first involves saying something to herself; the second involves saying something to the professor.

Remember the technique of silently repeating key sentences to yourself to combat the upstairs-downstairs effect? Opal can use the same technique here with great effectiveness. Opal can remind herself, "The department has made a mistake; I would have made a good teaching assistant," or, "The department's decision was not based on merit alone." And she can tell herself, "Whether or not I would be happy with the extra work is something I could have decided for myself."

By reminding herself of these things, Opal gains the distance from Professor O'Connors's comments necessary for her to sidestep the lessons they might otherwise teach her. At the same time, she uses the occasion of a remark that could be belittling to reinforce her sense of her own competence and maturity. As Opal begins to use this technique consistently, she turns each belittling remark made to her by a professor into a supportive and useful remark, simply by using it to remind herself of the inappropriateness of the intended message. You too can easily learn to make paternalistic remarks work for you, not against you.

The other thing Opal might want to do at the time of Professor O'Connors's comment is to say something to Professor O'Connors about it. She might say, for instance, "I appreciate your explaining the decision to me, though I would have preferred the opportunity to decide for myself whether it would be too much work for me.

Actually, I think that I could have handled the extra work quite easily.''

In all likelihood, it has simply not occurred to the professor that paternalism may be out of place here, or that the explanation offered could be anything other than a consolation to Opal. By pointing out to the professor what bothers her about it—assertively, not aggressively—Opal asks that he consider the appropriateness of paternalism critically. The professor may get the point. In any event, it is important for Opal to communicate her own views in a direct manner, both so that the professor has the opportunity to consider a side of the issue he might not have thought about, and also because speaking up in this way will help Opal establish and maintain her own constructive view of paternalism in the university.

The Value of Speaking Up

Speaking up is important in getting what you want in other ways, too. The "Problems" section discussed ways in which advisers or professors may steer you toward certain areas and away from others. The adviser may be motivated by a genuine concern for your well-being, but that view of what is good for you may be biased in various ways.

The first solution to this problem is simply to be critical in listening to advice given to you. Listen carefully to what your adviser tells you, and consider it fully. It may very well be useful. But you should always bear in mind the possibility that the adviser's recommendations are not really right for you. Don't overrate an adviser's counseling. If you are interested in a certain field, look into postgraduate possibilities on your own. You may turn up information that the adviser simply did not have.

The second solution is to speak up: tell your adviser what your interests are, and don't drop an important issue without properly discussing it. Arguing for your point of view can be a very useful way of sorting out the pros and cons of something you are considering, no matter what you decide to do in the end. In addition, you simply cannot blame the adviser for steering you in a certain direction if you have never made clear to the adviser which direction you have in mind.

The same point applies to the problem that Quintana faced in trying to find a campus job, and it applies to any dealings you may have with an employment or placement office concerning work as well. People who work in the placement office may have a hard time imagining women in certain jobs, or picturing them as being happy or productive in certain fields. *You have to tell them what your interests are.* Otherwise, you have yourself to blame if they fail to consider jobs in the areas you are interested in.

When Quintana was referred to the secretarial job, she could have asked whether there were any other sorts of work available. Or, when she learned of the research position, she could have gone back to the office and made further inquiries at that time. In all probability, the research position had not occurred to the person Quintana was talking to. But once Quintana mentioned this type of work, the person would have remembered the research job. In fact, Quintana could have prepared a short list of types of work she was interested in, and inquired concerning jobs in these areas first.

This point is probably even more important when you are looking for off-campus employment through your campus placement office. You must tell the people in the office clearly and directly what sorts of work you envision for yourself, and you must be prepared to be persistent if they are reluctant to refer you to jobs in those areas. People have habits of thought, and these habits can be slow to change. But you should simply not allow yourself to be steered by the habits of others in seeking employment. Usually all that is required in order to overcome the tendency others may have to steer you in certain ways is to point out, repeatedly if necessary, what it is that you want. At first, others may have a hard time hearing what you are saying, since it may not be what they expect you to say. Think of the problem as one of trying to communicate with someone whose language you don't speak very well. With a little patience and persistence, communication is almost always possible.

Another problem with Quintana's work-study job, aside from the fact of her having been steered to secretarial work, is the tendency that some people may still have to hire women for certain kinds of work and not for others. For the most part, this practice on campuses is guided by habits of thought and reinforced by the low visibility problem for women. For the most part, the solution remains the same: speak up. Tell people what you are interested in and what your qualifications are. Usually a little persistence is all that is required to secure a job that, without that persistence on your part, might have gone to a man simply because that has been the practice in the past.

For campus jobs that are advertised by word of mouth, low visibility results in an important aspect of the stacked-deck effect, since the practice makes it harder for women than for men to secure valuable forms of employment. Everything we've suggested for increasing your visibility and getting your job profile more highly evaluated works here, too. Let professors know what your interests and qualifications are. Let the Chair of your major department, or departments you are thinking of majoring in, know that you are interested in work *before* something comes up. This way, when a position does open up, the professor or Chair will think of you, and you will have a chance to hear about the job before it's filled.

We talked about the fact that the job Quintana was steered to received minimum wage, while the man who got a job the same week received a higher salary. We also talked about the possibility that students performing equivalent tasks might be hired under different job titles, in such a way that women would earn less than men. We have already discussed ways in which Quintana could have put herself in a better position to get a higher-paying job. Very similar points apply to seeing to it that you receive a fair wage for the work you do.

Don't be shy about asking for a raise. If you feel you are being underpaid for your work, mention the matter to your employer. Find out what job titles the other people working in your office have. If you do not want to discuss this matter with your office mates, or if, as may well be the case, they don't know what their job titles are, then you can check with the Office of Student Employment. There you should find a written record of student-held positions on campus, official job descriptions, and salary levels. If you have reason to believe that someone who is doing the same or comparable work to what you do is being paid more than you, discuss this with your supervisor. In many cases, it will simply not have occurred to her that the job descriptions are inequitable.

However, it is always possible that a problem you have, whether it concerns academic work, a job, or the salary you receive for that job, is not a simple result of the stacked-deck effect. There are problems related to those we have been discussing that do not respond to the techniques we have offered for increasing your visibility and job profile evaluations. These will be problems of sex discrimination proper. It is not the responsibility of the undergraduate to monitor and correct sex discrimination on campus. This is the job of certain governmental agencies and the responsibility of the university administration.

Nevertheless, it may occasionally happen that a student becomes aware that she is being discriminated against on the basis of gender. If you have any reason to believe that a professor, administrator, or department is discriminating against you in a matter concerning academic awards, appointments, or on-campus employment, then we refer you to Get Smart Course 404 for a discussion of sex discrimination on the college campus.

Solutions Summary

- Review the solutions offered in Get Smart Courses 101 and 202; learn to cultivate high visibility in the classroom and to teach the counter-curriculum.
- Compare notes with other students on which classes are teaching the hidden curriculum, and work particularly hard to teach the counter-curriculum in those classes where the hidden curriculum is being most obviously offered.
- Supply professors and department Chairs with the information they will need in order to give a fair evaluation of your job profile; let them know what your interests and plans are and what your employment qualifications are, including your financial need, if that is a factor.
- Prepare and periodically update your resume, and distribute it to the professors and department Chairs whose work or field interests you.
- Learn to recognize paternalistic remarks and to counteract them. Repeat key phrases to yourself that contradict paternalistic messages and point out paternalism to professors who engage in it; in the process, you undercut the practice of paternalistic decision making.
- Remember that the university is not a perfect meritocracy: decision making involves complex sorts of evaluations, which may reflect considerations unrelated to you personally and reward things that have little to do with intellectual talent.
- Be critical of advice given to you. Take it seriously, but consider the full range of your options, and seek information on things that interest you beyond what your adviser may offer.
- When seeking employment, speak up! Let advisers or employment counselors know what sort of jobs you are interested in and qualified for.
- See to it that you are paid a fair wage for the work you do; make sure that your job description is appropriate to your work, and speak with your supervisor if you think there is any disparity between what you're doing and what you're getting paid for.

Finally, if increasing your visibility and speaking up—with professors, advisers, job counselors, or employers—does not alleviate a problem, then read on to Get Smart Course 404. The "Solutions" section of that chapter explains the various offices and officers of the university who can help you if you meet with a problem that you can't solve on your own.

Get Smart
Course 404

University Policies: Increasing Your Opportunities When Policies Get Set

This chapter focuses on university policy. Policies that present academic obstacles to women in college are discriminatory, and the elimination of sex discrimination on campus is the appropriate responsibility of the campus administration. The "Solutions" section introduces the various offices and officers of the university available to assist you if you run into sex discrimination on campus.

Problems

There will be times when it is neither possible nor necessarily appropriate for students to remedy problems of discriminatory impact on their own. The problem of job descriptions discussed at the end of the previous chapter provides a useful illustration. Suppose that Quintana had gone to work in her office under the job title Clerk Typist, and then discovered that one of her male office mates was performing the same tasks under the title Office Assistant, at a higher wage. Suppose also that Quintana had discussed the matter with her supervisor.

The previous chapter suggested that this discussion would probably be all it would take to straighten out the problem. To the extent that this is true, the problem is a result of the stacked-deck effect. Clearly, it was in Quintana's case, since merely by "playing her cards right"—in this case, speaking up—she was able to solve the problem.

But suppose that Quintana's talk with her supervisor did not result in an adjustment of the office pay practices. In this case, there would be nothing more Quintana could do on her own. The university office for which Quintana was working would be engaging in sex discrimination, assuming that there were no mitigating circumstances. They would be paying Quintana less than a male worker performing the same tasks. This practice is illegal, and the university administration is responsible for seeing to it that such practices do not take place on campus. It would be both necessary and fully appropriate for Quintana to seek the assistance of someone from the university administration in correcting the problem.

Quintana's problem illustrates how some of the results of the stacked-deck effect are in and of themselves not distinguishable from the results of sex discrimination. However, specific problems resulting from the stacked-deck effect are usually fruitfully and appropriately dealt with by the students affected, although other people in the university community should also be concerned with combating these problems.

Any inequity in the education or employment of women on campus that is not fully remedied by measures of the sort discussed in Get Smart Course 303 (measures the student can undertake on her own) is a matter of sex discrimination and is best handled by the university administration. This chapter looks at some areas in which an undergraduate may encounter sex discrimination and describes in detail the various offices of the university that can be of assistance in overcoming discrimination on campus.

Campus Safety

To begin, consider one aspect of college that you may not think of as affecting your education at all: the campus itself. Whether your college is in a major city or in the country, whether it has an enclosed campus or consists of buildings spread out across a large area, there are certain features of the campus that are invariant.

For instance, at certain hours most campus buildings are quiet and empty, while at other times the whole campus is teeming with people. People tend to walk certain routes at certain times of day on certain days of the week, in order to get to particular classes and other activities from the dormitories, or from public transportation stops and parking lots. The campus offers different types of routes: to get to one class, you cut across a lawn; to get to the dining hall, you cross a parking lot or walk through a basement tunnel. Particularly if you live on an urban or a large, sprawling campus, there are certain forms of public transportation that are routinely and predictably used to get to and from campus buildings.

You may never think about the campus and its patterns, but that doesn't mean that you aren't dealing with them on a day-to-day basis. Do you tend to avoid very deserted or very crowded areas of the campus when walking alone? Do you take into consideration how you are going to get home from a nighttime concert, lecture, meeting, or social event when deciding whether to attend it? Do you prefer to avoid classes given at night or early in the morning, when the campus is relatively deserted? Do you ever double-check to make sure you've locked your dorm room door at night before you go to sleep?

In all of these ways and many others, students plan their time and activities around aspects of the campus environment to which they devote little explicit thought. Moreover, these are all ways that women may allow their activities to be affected by the campus environment but that men do not. Men are far less likely to worry about getting home before they decide whether to go out at night, or to avoid certain paths or certain classes out of caution.

There is a good reason why women allow their decisions in certain areas to be influenced by the campus in these ways. Women, and not men, must exercise caution in their daily dealings with the campus environment because women, and not men, can be raped. That is, there is one form of violent crime that women must take precautions against when planning their activities, which men need not. Hence the campus itself can be experienced differently, and have different effects on, the day-to-day lives of women and men.

This difference that women and men have in the experience of the campus is an educational issue. To see why this is so, let's consider an example.

Rani is taking an introductory astronomy course that has weekly homework assignments. Once a week a session is led by a teaching assistant to go over the homework problems. The problem sessions are scheduled at 8:00 A.M. in the science building. The science building has several wings, and in order to get to the classroom, Rani must walk down long corridors and through doors at the end of each. At that hour of the day, the building is almost completely empty. Around the third time that Rani attends the problem session, one of the doors she needs to pass through has not yet been unlocked for the day. Rani finds herself at the end of a long, deserted hallway, in front of a locked door. Rani retraces her steps, and in a couple of minutes she meets the security guard who is coming to unlock the door. But Rani is not inclined to attend the next few sessions.

Rani found the experience of being confronted by the locked door spooky and unsettling. Her avoidance of the problem sessions thereafter may be a conscious decision on her part, or may simply result from the unease that she now associates with getting to the room where the sessions are held. In either case, Rani's avoidance of the problem sessions is reasonable. It would be unwise for her to put herself in a position where at a predictable time on a certain day of the week, she can be found standing alone at the end of a long, empty corridor, sometimes in front of a locked door. It is reasonable for Rani to be cautious under the circumstances. Her safety comes before her attendance at the sessions.

If Rani stops attending the problem sessions, she will be exercising reasonable judgment in being cautious. But from the educational point of view, she is missing out on an important opportunity. The problem sessions are an important part of the astronomy class. It may be that Rani is missing an aspect of the class that cannot be replaced by any other arrangement, since the discussions that go on in those sessions occur between students and the teaching assistant in the context of the sessions arranged for just that purpose.

Although it is Rani's *decision* not to attend the next few problem sessions, this does not mean that she is *responsible* for depriving herself of this educational opportunity. The hour at which the problem session is scheduled, combined with the particulars of the building in which it is held, make it inadvisable for Rani to continue attending. Her educational activities are being restricted by aspects of her campus environment.

Furthermore, Rani's activities are being restricted because she is a woman. A man finding himself at the end of the hall confronted by a locked door will not find it spooky or unsettling in the way or to the extent that Rani does, and will be unlikely to curtail his attendance on the basis of this experience. This is not because Rani is too sensitive or immature about the experience. It is because a danger exists for Rani that simply does not exist for a man. Everything in Rani's upbringing has led her to be especially wary of such situations. But this is in part because such situations pose a special threat to her.

The fact that Rani curtails her attendance at the problem sessions as a result of this experience reflects one way in which the campus itself can affect the educational opportunities of women. In a certain sense, the hour at which the problem session takes place and the building in which it meets stack the deck against Rani: they make it more difficult for her than it would be for a man to secure the educational opportunity that the problem sessions offer. But neither the scheduling of classes nor campus security is properly Rani's responsibility.

There are several ways in which considerations essentially similar to those in Rani's case can serve to restrict the access women have to certain educational opportunities. Some women avoid signing up for classes scheduled to meet at night. They may worry about the walk home afterward, or the necessity of taking public transportation home at that hour. Sometimes alternative sections of a class may be held during the day. But sometimes there is no real alternative to a class that is offered at night.

In some cases the class may be required, or it may be a prerequisite for other classes. The student who tries to avoid such a course altogether, or who postpones it in the hope that it will be given during the day at some point in the future, is being deprived of an educational opportunity on the basis of gender.

Notice that this will be a particular problem for part-time students, since many of their courses will be offered only at night. Since part-time students tend to work during the day, the consideration of nighttime safety can make it more difficult for a woman to attend college part-time than for a man. Since older students, returning to school after many years of work or raising families, often return on a part-time basis, this can mean that it is more difficult for the older woman to return to school than for the older man. In all of these

ways, the necessity for caution can restrict women's access to educational opportunities.

In the same way, women might need to curtail their use of the
campus library. Since most classes are held during the day, evening
and weekend hours may provide the best chances for pursuing research in the library. However, nighttime use of the library may
involve walks across campus or the use of public transportation at
night, and weekend use of the libraries may mean empty areas of
the building, for example, in rooms containing study carrels. Thus,
safety precautions can lead to reduced access for women, but not for
men, to the educational opportunities provided by extended use of
the campus libraries.

Other university facilities may also offer this problem for women.
Undergraduates may find themselves unable to use a computer center during the peak day hours, when graduate students as well are
competing for computer time. As a result, it may be educationally
valuable to be able to use the computer center at night. Particularly
if the computer center is not well populated at night, or if transportation to and from the center is a problem, women may in effect
have reduced access to this educational resource. The same may be
true of various pieces of laboratory equipment that are shared by
many students.

Similar considerations apply to the access women have to the many
cultural and social events offered on campus. Lectures, concerts,
films, discussion groups, and parties all tend to be scheduled at night.
Similarly, access to the gym may be affected. Women's ability to take
advantage of these opportunities may thus be hindered as well.

The problems posed for women by these various instances of the
need to place safety ahead of educational advantage vary in the degree of their severity and in the locus of responsibility for their alleviation. Different campuses present different instances of the
problems, and different problems will be handled in different ways,
if at all. Some of these problems can be handled by stepped-up security in certain areas or at certain times. This is the responsibility
of the university administration. Sometimes the professor or graduate student who is in charge of assigning computer time or access to
some piece of equipment will be making it more difficult for women
to gain access to the resource by unnecessarily scheduling it for
nighttime hours. In such cases, it is the responsibility of the department head to see to it that such practices stop.

Employment

Just as precautionary considerations may hinder you from attending certain events or restrict your access to certain places, caution may be a factor in seeking employment on campus as well. Common sense may dictate that a woman not accept a job checking student ID's at night, for example, although such work offers minimal interference with class time and a good chance to study while earning money. Hence, one very desirable form of employment from the educational point of view may be effectively less accessible to women than to men. A similar point might apply to work involving monitoring an experiment at night.

In such cases, women's access to campus work may be restricted as a result of certain aspects of the work itself. There are other ways in which women's access to work may be restricted that are not the result of anything intrinsic to the work, as in the following example.

Sheila is looking for a job. She finds this advertisement posted on the bulletin board of the Office of Student Employment:

Part-time help wanted. Laboratory Assistant needed to work on a chemistry project. No laboratory experience necessary; applicants must have taken at least one year of college calculus.

Since Sheila has not taken calculus, she does not bother to apply for the position.

There is nothing in this job advertisement that prohibits women from holding the job. Nevertheless, since it turns out that fewer women than men take a full year of college calculus, in fact, the calculus requirement makes it harder for women to qualify, as a rule, than for men.

It is conceivable that calculus will really be necessary for the work. It is also conceivable that it will not be. For example, the assistant's responsibilities might be limited to setting up, monitoring, and cleaning equipment; the job might never involve numerical calculations of any sort. In this case, Sheila is dissuaded from applying for, and perhaps barred from holding down, a job that she is fully qualified to do.

If calculus is not required for the work itself, then this advertisement constitutes a form of sex discrimination recognized by the law as *disproportionate impact. A practice that is not overtly discriminatory, but that has disproportionate effects on women relative to men, may constitute sex discrimination in the legal sense.* In this case, if it is true that mastery of first-year calculus is irrelevant to the work that will be required of the student, then, since fewer women than men complete one year of calculus, the advertisement discriminates against women.

Many of the problems discussed in Get Smart Course 303 are in essence problems of disproportionate impact. It is not fruitful to think of them as cases of sex discrimination, since their causes are straightforward and their solutions simple. Merely speaking up, discussing them in a direct way with the people involved, is generally enough to overcome them. It makes more sense to think of the sorts of problems that arise from safety considerations as involving disproportionate impact. When these problems involve the provision of security on campus, or the scheduling of classes, the responsibility for ensuring that the disproportionate impact on women is minimalized lies not with the individual student but with the university administration.

At the same time, insofar as safety considerations can result in various university policies having disproportionate educational impact on women, it may become necessary for students to approach campus officials in order to initiate the elimination of discriminatory aspects of those policies. It is therefore important to learn to recognize practices that have a disproportionate impact on women, and to learn to assess which office of the university has the responsibility to correct them.

The job advertisement we just looked at involves disproportionate impact on women, not simply because it is a result of the stacked-deck effect but because it is the result of somebody's stacking the deck against women—namely, the person who wrote the job description for the advertisement. The person responsible may not be aware of the discriminatory nature of the advertisement. In this case, the student could point out the fact that calculus is not necessary to do the work and thereby convince the person to change the ad. More likely, however, the student will not be in a position to recognize the discriminatory nature of the advertisement, since she is not likely to know what is actually needed for the work. This is nevertheless a case of sex discrimination in the form of disproportionate impact, and it is the responsibility of the university administration to put a stop to such practices.

Many of the employment problems examined in Get Smart Course 303 can shade off from the stacked-deck effect to become problems of sex discrimination. A particular adviser or job counselor may refuse to refer you for certain jobs on the grounds that women are not suited to the work. Or a particular on-campus employer may refuse to give you a job because the employer prefers not to hire a woman. These practices are illegal. The university administration has a responsibility to be sure they do not go on, and the student confronted with such discrimination should solicit the help of the appropriate officers of the university. Even in the case of an off-campus employer who hires students and engages in sex discrimination, there are certain measures that campus officers should take. For example, the placement office can stop posting such an employer's job announcements.

It is not likely, even if you are being discriminated against in employment, that you will be in a position to know that it is happening, or to substantiate your claim to an administrator. Employers are unlikely to give you their reasons for not giving you a job and, if they did, would not give you reasons that directly reflect discrimination. *If you encounter a problem that has the characteristic features of the stacked-deck effect but that does not respond to the methods discussed in Get Smart Course 303 for overcoming it, then you may be encountering sex discrimination.*

For example, suppose that Quintana did not get an adequate response when she dealt with the problem of salary discrepancies in her office as an instance of the stacked-deck effect. She would then have to consider the possibility that she was encountering sex discrimination and begin pursuing the remedies for it that are discussed in the "Solutions" section of this chapter.

Other Areas of Discrimination

There are also other areas in which sex discrimination can occur. It is important for you to be aware that the possibility of discrimination exists so that you can recognize it if it does come up and know which office of the university has the responsibility to correct it.

While universities have become more careful to avoid overtly discriminatory practices, individual professors and administrators may in some cases be slower to learn. There are still some professors who explicitly engage in discrimination against women. For example, a male professor might systematically discourage women from enrolling in his courses. Some discouragement may take the form of insulting remarks, either in private or in class, to the effect that women are unfit for participation in the field. Some professors still attempt to prevent women from enrolling in classes or from working on certain laboratory projects. Tammy has this problem with a male forestry professor.

Tammy's forestry class, in which she is the only female student, is preparing for a weekend field trip to a nearby tract of forest, to collect soil and plant samples for subsequent analysis. The professor is assigning tasks for each of the students to perform during the trip, but he neglects to assign a task to Tammy. When she inquires, the professor makes clear that he has assumed that she will not be going on the trip. When she says that she plans to go with the rest of the class, he warns her, "No one's going to carry you back to the bus the first time a snake crosses your path!" He suggests that there is some relevant reading she could do instead, which could be useful to the class later on, and that she will be better off in the library than in the woods.

Fieldwork is important to the study of forestry, and Tammy is being deprived of an educational opportunity. The professor's idea that Tammy should provide background research work instead of picking up valuable practical experience is not something that Tammy should accept.

Various clubs and campus social groups can offer instances of sex discrimination as well. These groups may be organized in such a way as to bar women from participation, or in such a way that it is hard for women to hold offices or other important positions within the organization. In addition to the immediate benefits of participation, graduate and professional schools and employers may weigh such participation in a student's favor. These clubs can also offer valuable connections for postgraduate work. In these ways, the structure of student organizations can contribute to disproportionate impact on women.

Funding from the college may also be inequitably distributed to organizations run by or for women. The distribution of funds to campus groups differs from school to school and is dependent on the nature of the group, the campus agency responsible for the distribution of funds, and the source of the funds.

Other sorts of inequities, while they are diminishing in the wake of the Education Amendments of 1972 (see Get Smart Course 505), are still to be found. Athletic facilities on campus may not be equivalent for women and men. The women's athletic equipment may not meet the standards of the men's. Women's teams may receive less funding, and therefore not be able to afford full-time coaching staffs, adequate sports equipment, or transportation to away games. Women's practice sessions may be restricted to less desirable times, before or after the men's teams have had their workouts. Or women may simply be barred from participation in certain sports.

In addition, men's teams may have trainers available to help with injuries or other sports-related problems, while the women's teams may not. This means, in effect, that the men are receiving a form of health coverage while participating in sports that the women do not. Health insurance policies may contribute to this problem as well, if they protect against certain health problems only when they result from campus sports activities. A campus where women tend to participate less actively than men in organized sports may in this way offer a health insurance policy with disproportionate impact on women.

Another area in which health coverage may be discriminatory concerns pregnancy. The law now requires pregnancy to be given the same coverage as other forms of temporary disabilities, but not all student health insurance plans do so. In addition, some campuses may offer inadequate gynecological and birth control services. For a discussion of legal requirements in this area, the reader is referred to Get Smart Course 505.

Other areas that can offer discrimination or disproportionate impact on women include admissions and financial aid. Because the mechanisms of decision making in these areas are seldom visible to the undergraduate, and because the undergraduate is not responsible for alleviating problems in these areas, they are not discussed here. References to this subject may be found in the bibliography at the end of the book.

Certain groups of women may experience greater sex discrimination on campus than others. Black women, for example, may be the subject of sex discrimination compounded by racial discrimination which results in a discriminatory college environment for them that is greater than the sum of its parts. This can be true as well for women who are members of other minorities, for older women, for lesbians, and for women with disabilities.

Different Treatment versus Discriminatory Treatment

The law does not require treatment of women and men to be identical in order for it to meet the requirements of being nondiscriminatory. For example, colleges are not required to provide identical amounts of funding for women's and men's sports teams. What they are required to provide is equivalent funding relative to student interest. A college that has a large and well-funded men's football team is not required to invest an equal number of dollars in women's football, or even in women's sports in general. What is required is that, where the interest exists, the women's teams be funded in proportion to their attendance as well as the men's teams, and that the women not be deprived of advantages held by the men in campus-funded sports activities. Putting this in concrete terms can be difficult. But what should be noted is that this is a case in which the law recognizes treatment of women that is different from treatment of men (in this case, the policies may differ in the dollar amounts committed to women's and men's teams) as nondiscriminatory.

The legal requirement regarding pregnancy coverage in health insurance illustrates another aspect of this point. The law specifically addresses the issue of pregnancy. This is a matter that directly affects women, and not men. However, in mentioning pregnancy a health insurance policy is not discriminatory, although it applies to women and not to men, since women start off in a different position than men relative to the policy. In this case, the difference is strictly biological: women, and not men, can become pregnant. Hence the law requires the college health coverage to include a provision that applies only to women, because in this case not to do so would be discriminatory. The law requires pregnancy to be treated like any other temporary disability, on the grounds that if it weren't, then, given the biological difference between women and men, women would in effect be discriminated against.

Both of these examples illustrate ways in which treatment of women that differs from treatment of men, or policies that apply to women and not to men, may be recognized by the law as nondiscriminatory. In fact, a great many of the problems discussed in Get Smart Course 303 and in this chapter are illustrations of ways in which policies that fail to treat women and men differently can be discriminatory in their effects.

For example, when faculty consider class participation in decisions concerning grades, awards, or teaching assistantships, they may in effect be discriminating against women. If women, for whatever reasons, find it harder than men to participate actively in classroom discussion, then, although nothing in the faculty's criteria explicitly gives an advantage to men, women will in fact have a harder time winning the advantages the faculty is meting out.

Similarly, if women have a harder time than men in securing research-related employment, then a department that gives preference to students who hold research positions when making financial aid decisions, for instance, is in effect discriminating against women. Nothing in the department's decision making may explicitly make the requirements harder for women to meet than for men to meet. But the failure to compensate in any way for the disadvantageous position that women start out in results in one form of discrimination.

It is common, but mistaken, to identify *different* treatment with *discriminatory* treatment. Many people argue that any policy that treats women and men differently is discriminatory. This may be true in cases where women and men start off in equal circumstances relative to the policy. But in cases in which they do not, policies that fail to consider and compensate for differences in their starting positions may in fact have discriminatory impact on women.

It is sometimes necessary to adopt policies that explicitly treat women differently from men in order not to discriminate against them. The relationship between being different and being discriminatory is sometimes a complicated one. There are cases in which identical treatment is highly discriminatory. There are others in which different treatment is highly equitable.

There is one very important area in which women face circumstances that are not identical to those faced by men, and that is the one we started off this chapter discussing: campus safety. Because there is a form of violent attack to which women, and not men, are vulnerable on campus, it may be that security policies that treat women and men identically have disproportionate impact on women. Furthermore, the issue of safety on campus is also an issue of educational opportunity for women. Therefore, it may be that in order not to discriminate against women educationally, college administrations have a responsibility for the security for women on campus that differs from their responsibility for men. Let's examine in a little more detail why this might be so.

Rape

Rape is an undeniable fact of life in every community across the United States. The college campus offers no haven from this violent crime. A 1974 survey conducted by the Center for Women's Policy Studies for the National Institute of Law Enforcement shows that college rape is not concentrated on urban campuses. The survey shows that rape occurs on all college campuses in the United States—urban, suburban, and rural alike—at rates ranging from one to twelve rapes per campus per year. Parking lots and garages, poorly lit open spaces and narrow paths, empty academic buildings, library stacks, deserted laundry rooms, and campus basements all make for high-risk areas. In addition, the high concentration of women, many traveling predictable paths as part of their daily routines, means that rape is a fact of life on the college campus. Accurate statistics on the incidence of rape are hard to compile, since rape is the most underreported of all violent crimes. It is believed that as few as one out of every ten rapes is reported to the police. In addition, so-called date rape is probably the most underreported type of rape. *Date rape* refers to forced intercourse by an acquaintance, generally someone the victim is seeing socially. Since many women still fail to consider intercourse against their will with a date or casual acquaintance as rape, the frequency of date rape is very difficult to assess.

One factor contributing to both the incidence and the underreporting of rape is the long-standing tradition on college campuses of women allowing themselves to be pressured into pursuing sexual relations with men. A woman may feel that, having agreed to a date, or perhaps even having flirted with a man, she owes him whatever he wants. She may feel that she is being rude when she tries to say no, or that she has no right to refuse him something he wants. She may simply feel incapable of saying no loudly and clearly enough.

Fortunately, this tradition is being eroded. More and more women are recognizing their own preferences and their own rights to do as they want, not as their male friends want. But the tendency to be deferential to men simply because they are men still survives in many of us. This is something that has to change.

Whenever a man puts pressure on you to engage in sexual activities that you do not wish to engage in—even when the setting is social, even when you yourself have carried the flirtation to a certain point—that man's behavior is out of line. He is, however unwittingly, exploiting your probable tendency to be deferential to him, and posing a threat to induce you into sexual intimacy.

Rape is an educational issue on college campuses. There are two reasons that this is so. First, the very possibility that women can be raped on campus can affect their educations in the ways discussed at the beginning of this chapter. The need to exercise caution and to consider personal safety in making decisions about courses to take, times to use the libraries, and what jobs to take make it more difficult for women to secure the same educational advantages that men have.

In addition, some forms of educational resources may be effectively less accessible to women, for instance, if they cannot get adequate daytime access to a computer, or to certain pieces of equipment. The various forms of social and cultural events that college life offers may also be less accessible to women than men. And these too play a crucial role in the total education of the student. In all of these ways, the fact that women are different from men has an adverse effect on their educations because, social circumstances being what they are, women must exercise special cautions against rape.

The second reason that rape is an educational issue pertains to the fact that a woman who has been raped has been victimized, and her victimization will affect her ability to learn and to perform effectively as a student. Rape is a violent crime, usually experienced by the victim as a life-threatening attack. As is the case with all victims of sudden, violent events, including car crashes, for example, the victim of rape has undergone a shock from which it takes time to recover.

The student who is raped must recover from the shock of being attacked. In addition, she will have many immediate problems to confront. In the weeks that follow the rape, the victim will have to make decisions about whether to tell her parents, her friends, or her boyfriend. In cases of date rape, where the rapist may be a member of a circle of her friends, this may be especially difficult. She may worry about being pregnant, or having caught a venereal disease or AIDS. She may wonder whether to press legal charges. And it will take time to regain her sense of control over her life and to regain some ease with her own judgment and daily activities.

In the aftermath of a rape, the victim is likely to encounter difficulties in her studies. The normal recovery pattern for shock involves a period of numbness or disengagement, followed by a period of depression, before the immediate emotional effects subside. During these periods, the victim may have an understandably difficult time concentrating on schoolwork. She may also be anxious about the area of the campus where the rape occurred, or about her ability to get around campus in safety. This may curtail her use of the libraries, reduce her class attendance, and diminish her use of other educational opportunities as well.

Many campuses have already developed comprehensive rape prevention programs, and many have victim services care. Women do recover from rape, and a woman who has been raped can go on to be a fully productive and outstanding student. But the fact is that it can take time before the student is ready to return her full attentions to her studies. In the interim, it is possible for her grades to drop a bit and for her academic education to be temporarily interrupted.

Since women, and not men, can be raped on campus, this means that the campus offers an impediment to higher education for women—both for women as a group, insofar as reason dictates certain safety precautions, and for the individual victim of rape, whose academic education can be disrupted by the crime. Particularly in cases where a temporary drop in grades or an abrupt temporary leave of absence can later be held against the student when decisions are made concerning teaching assistantships, financial aid, or entrance to graduate or professional school, these features of campus life may impede not only a student's educational progress but her professional or postgraduate progress as well.

It is the responsibility of the college administration to minimalize the risk of rape on campus, and to ensure that the campus rape victim has all the resources she needs to assist her in recovering from the attack. This includes minimalizing the possible educational consequences of such an attack; a sudden, temporary drop in grades, for instance, should not be given too much weight in evaluating the student's overall record. Failure to address the issue of rape on campus on the part of the college administration can result, in essence, in a form of discrimination against women. In this case, it may turn out that *failure* to treat women differently in certain ways—for example, by not providing them with special campus security—can result in sex discrimination by the college.

Solutions

The common thread that ties together the discriminatory practices discussed in this chapter is that their resolution is properly the responsibility of the university administration. While the individual student may wish to become involved in the alleviation of problems of discrimination on campus, it is not her responsibility as a student to do so. If she encounters discrimination that impedes her educational progress, then it is the administration's responsibility to correct it. What you need to know, in case you encounter sex discrimination in the course of your college education, is whom to approach on campus for assistance and the most fruitful way to go about it.

This section is organized a bit differently from the previous "Solutions" sections. Instead of looking at each case from the "Problems" section, this chapter presents a set of procedures that should be followed in approaching the administration on any of the problems discussed. Since any of the problems noted so far in this book can develop into a problem of sex discrimination, this section actually presents procedures for dealing with these problems once the remedies already suggested have been exhausted. Therefore, this section is not limited to the problems explicitly discussed in this chapter.

Get Smart Course 303 showed how habits of thought and patterns of social interaction could create the stacked-deck effect, and how the problems discussed in Get Smart Courses 101 and 202 were in a sense the principal ingredients of the stacked-deck effect. Thus the solutions discussed in the first three chapters were for the most part ways in which a student could even out the odds on her own, or together with other students. In many cases, a practice that appears to be sex discrimination is really no more than the stacked-deck effect. For example, in Quintana's office where the salaries are inequitable, it may be that all Quintana needs to do is discuss the problem with her supervisor. She may need to be persistent, and she should be prepared to argue her case for a raise. But if the supervisor changes Quintana's job description so as to make it equitable as a result of her having pointed out the problem, then Quintana knows the problem was a simple matter of the stacked-deck effect. For various reasons, the supervisor may have had a hard time seeing that the pay practices in the office had been inequitable, but once it was pointed out clearly and directly, the supervisor corrected the practice.

In general, whenever you feel that you have been denied some advantage or been turned down for some position on grounds that are unfair, the first thing to do is to act as if you are confronting the stacked-deck effect. Talk to your supervisor, professor, or department head. Ask about the grounds for the decision. Point out ways in which the decision may have been unwittingly "stacked." Tell people what your interests and preferences are. Point out inequitable hiring and pay practices. Chances are good that you can even out the odds simply by speaking up and undertaking the measures we suggested for increasing your visibility.

So, when attempting to solve a problem you are having on campus that you suspect may be related to your being a woman, the first rule to follow is: *Treat your problem as if it were a case of the stacked-deck effect. Do not consider the problem to be a matter of sex discrimination unless your attempts to handle it by talking directly to the people involved have failed to produce adequate results.*

Now, *if* you have tried talking to the people involved about the problem, and *if* the responses you have met with have not been adequate and the problem has not been solved, *then and only then* should you consider thinking of the problem as a problem of sex discrimination. At this point, you should try to figure out whether your problem is one that should be taken up with the administration. The first thing you need to assess this possibility is a reasonably concise statement of the problem.

Defining the Problem and Solution
When stating the problem, try to be as specific and as local as the problem and its solution require. Quintana's problem, for instance, is that her salary level is not as high as that of another worker in the

same office who shares the same job responsibilities. Of course, in a
sense, Quintana's problem is a matter of sex discrimination only
insofar as it is part of a pattern of women receiving lower wages
than men for comparable work. But if Quintana wants to approach
the administration with the problem of inequitable salary policies
generally, then she won't get very far. Quintana herself is faced with
a specific obstacle: her salary inequity. This requires a specific solution: a salary adjustment. Of course, not all of the discriminatory
problems you may experience are as simply and locally statable as
Quintana's problem.

*In general, your problem—the one you want the administration to help
you with—is not sexual harassment on campuses across the country, or
wage discrimination in the United States. Your problem is a more specific
instance of harassment or discrimination. If you want the administration's assistance, you need to be able to state your problem in manageable
terms.*

There is one very important exception to this rule. We will return
to it later, but it is worth noting here. It may be that you observe
some pattern of difficulties women face in your school, or in connection with a particular class, department, or school activity. In this
case, you may want to approach the administration primarily for the
purpose of calling attention to the problem. If your intention is to
increase awareness of a problem, rather than to effect a specific solution to a problem that you yourself are immediately confronted
with, then a more general statement of the problem may be appropriate.

Once you have a reasonably concise statement of the problem, you
can assess whether you ought to approach the administration with
it. To do that, ask yourself: What would constitute a solution to my
problem? Another way to put this is to ask: What is it that I would
like, ideally, for the administration to do about my problem? In some
cases, the answer to this question will be straightforward. For Quintana, for instance, a rephrasing of her job description in a way that
brings her salary in line with her male office mate's salary would be
a solution. She needs to find someone in the university who will see
to it that this is done.

In other cases, this may be more difficult. Suppose, like Opal, you
have been turned down for a teaching assistantship, and you have
grounds to believe that your sports participation was weighted differently in the department's decision than it would have been for a
man. What would constitute a solution to your problem? Would you
want the administration to insist that the department give you an
assistantship?

This might indeed be the fairest resolution of the situation. But, in fact, if you succeeded in getting the administration to insist that the department give you a job, the results would probably not be what you would have wanted. The faculty members of the department, resenting the administration's interference in what they see as their arena, would in all likelihood supply a credible list of reasons why you were not fit to hold the job, and that would be the end of that. In addition, you would face the department's hostility for your action.

In some cases, the fair resolution is impossible. That is one reason why the techniques in Get Smart Course 303 for raising your visibility are so vital; they *prevent* the problem. After the fact, solutions may be impossible in specific cases. Once the decision has been made, you might still want to approach the administration about changing patterns of discrimination against women in that department. In fact, a group of women from the department might want to do this together. But the solution to your particular problem—not having a teaching assistantship—is not something that the administration is likely to be able to help you with in the case described here.

So, you must have a specific description of your problem, and it should be as narrowly defined as possible. And you should have as clear an idea as possible of what it is that you want the administration to do. In principle, how the problem is to be solved should also be the administration's concern. But if you don't know what you want from them, you are not likely to be successful in your dealings with them.

The problem might be: My salary is not commensurate with the work I am doing, as measured by the salary of my office mate. The solution: My job description needs to be reassessed.

The problem might be: Women in our department never or rarely get teaching assistantships. The solution: Administration assistance in evaluating and redesigning decision procedures in the department.

The problem might be: The officers of this college-funded club are required to play on varsity teams. Since there are more men's varsity sports here than women's, it is harder for women than for men to become officers. The solution: Change the club rules.

The important thing to bear in mind when deciding whether or not to approach the administration with a particular problem is that there must

*be some possible outcome of your talks with administrators that would
constitute a solution to the problem.*

Approaching the Administration

Assuming that you have stated your problem and decided that there
is a possible outcome to talking with the administration that would
constitute a solution to it, you now need to know which office in the
administration to approach. The college is organized hierarchically,
with offices at the lower end of the system having only local authority and offices higher up having authority over groups of lower offices. *The principle to follow in approaching the administration is always
start at the bottom of the system and work your way up only as this
becomes necessary.*

This principle is important for two reasons. The first is that the
simpler the solution to your problem, the better. And the fewer offices involved in affecting the solution, the simpler it is. The second
reason is that no administrator will "go over the head" of another,
unless there are extraordinary grounds for doing so. That is, virtually
anyone you come in contact with while trying to solve your problem
will want to be sure that you have observed protocol, meaning that
you have already attempted to resolve your problem with administrators lower in the campus hierarchy. If you haven't, the office you are
in will not undertake any action. This is what's known as following
channels. It's something you will have to accommodate yourself to.

One exception to this is the case in which your primary motivation
for talking with administration is to bring some situation to the administration's attention. In such a case, where the person you speak
to is not being asked to do anything immediately, it may not be
necessary to follow channels.

Depending on whether your problem is academic, employment-
related, or some other type of problem, the sequence of offices in
the relevant hierarchy will differ. Academic problems are those concerning grades; Honors; the awarding of jobs based on academic
merit, such as teaching assistantships; letters of recommendation;
and other matters of this sort. Employment matters include hiring
and wage decisions and employment counseling by university officers
or professors. The category of "other" includes sports; university-
sponsored clubs; and security.

For academic problems, you should contact offices in the following
order: department head or Director of Undergraduate Studies; Dean
of Students; a higher-level dean (such as dean of academic affairs) or
the Office of Affirmative Action. For employment problems, the or-

der is: supervisor; employment or work-study office; then Dean of Students or Office of Affirmative Action. For other problems, first contact the program or services director (such as Director of Health Services or Director of Athletics); then the Dean of Students or the Office of Affirmative Action. If your campus has an ombudsperson, it is appropriate to contact that person at any point in the sequence.

Remember, before you begin to work your way up the hierarchy for any type of problem, the first step is to talk directly with the person or people involved. The next step is to talk with that person's immediate supervisor. In academic matters, the lowest administrative position is department Chair. The adjustment of course schedules, from evening to daytime for instance, is an appropriate sort of problem to approach the department Chair with. Occasionally, the department may have a Director of Undergraduate Studies as well, and you may wish to approach this person first. You can find out from the departmental secretary which professor has administrative responsibilities for the department or for the undergraduate program in the department. Another easy way to find out who is serving in these capacities is by checking the college catalogue. Make sure you've got an up-to-date copy, however, since these positions tend to rotate fairly frequently.

In employment cases, the lowest administrative position is the supervisor of the office you work in. In cases where you are employed by a department, this person may just be the department Chair. If you have a work-study job, the first administrative office to go to is the work-study office.

In all other cases, after seeking solutions with the most immediately relevant individual on campus, you should go directly to the next higher administrative office in the hierarchy. A description of some of the key offices and administrative functions may prove helpful.

Dean of Students. Every college has a Dean of Students (or Student Affairs). It is part of that person's function to deal with the specific problems and difficulties of individual students. It should not be difficult to obtain an appointment with the Dean of Students or someone from the dean's office. The dean will generally have sufficient authority to effect some change to correct the problem. Thus, if the dean sympathizes with your perception of a problem or if you have succeeded in persuading her that there is a problem, you may get results.

There are some problems that the Dean of Students will clearly be interested in. One concerns course enrollments. Deans are always interested in raising course enrollments. If you have been denied

access to a course on the basis of your gender, explicitly or implic-
itly, the Dean of Students is an excellent person to consult. Or, if the
mere rescheduling of a course to another time would increase its
enrollment, and the department Chair has not given the change adequate consideration, then the dean is likely to be willing to take
this matter up with the department in question. Another sort of problem that may be fruitful to take up with the dean is one that has a
wide scope. For example, if you feel that women's sports are under-
represented or understaffed on your campus, or that a particular team
is missing, you should consider taking this up with the Dean of Students. Or, similarly, if you feel that there is insufficient women's
health coverage at the student health service, the dean's office is one
place to discuss your concerns and suggestions.

Along similar lines, it is appropriate to discuss the issue of safety
for women on campus with the Dean of Students. If there are some
measures on campus, such as early curfews for women, which pur-
port to address the issue of women's safety but which are in fact
detrimental to women's college experience, these should be brought
to the dean's attention. Or, if you have encountered specific safety
hazards, as did Rani, the dean could make the appropriate adjust-
ments. If there is no rape prevention or victim service program, this
is another topic to bring up with the dean.

Every campus administration is a bit idiosyncratic, but within the
Office of the Dean of Students on your campus, there will be some
sort of hierarchical administrative structure. The dean is likely to
have several assistant deans, for example. Thus it is quite possible
that when you first approach the dean's office, you will actually speak
with an assistant dean. If the assistant dean cannot help you or does
not sufficiently resolve your problem, then you must consult directly
with the dean.

There are risks to this approach, however. You have no assurance
of confidentiality in your conversations with the dean. The dean is
quite likely to discuss your case with other deans and administrators
and whomever else is relevant in order to investigate your claims or
to seek solutions to the problem. In some cases, such as problems
you may have had with specific departments or professors, this lack
of confidentiality may pose a problem. In addition, the Office of the
Dean of Students is not an independently functioning office on campus. Rather, the dean must report to other administrators in the college hierarchy. Thus the dean forms an integral part of the
administrative network which sets the policy on your campus. It is
not likely that you will find a sympathetic ear in the dean's office to

problems concerning discriminatory practices that result from this policy.

The Office of Affirmative Action. This office is set up in accordance with Title IX of the 1972 Education Amendments (see Get Smart Course 505). Under Title IX, every campus must have an Office of Affirmative Action designed to serve all students, staff, and faculty. The Affirmative Action Officer is on campus to hear all complaints of sex discrimination and harassment and to monitor the affirmative action and other anti-discrimination programs on campus. A major task of the Office of Affirmative Action, from the point of view of the university administration, is to protect the college from legal suits resulting from discriminatory practices on the campus.

Affirmative Action Officers are generally sympathetic toward the problems of women in higher education. Even more than the Dean of Students, the Affirmative Action Officer may be anxious to hear about issues and general circumstances on campus that pose educational roadblocks for women. Thus problems of safety on campus and sex discrimination in sports and health facilities are matters that the Affirmative Action Officer can try to mobilize the administration to act on. The officer will have access to descriptions of anti-discrimination programs that have been used at other colleges, and she can adapt them to your campus with the cooperation of the appropriate branches of the college.

When approaching the Affirmative Action Officer you should bear in mind the double-edged interests of the office. It is not an independent office but part of the Office of the President. The Affirmative Action Officer reports to members of the campus administration and works together with college deans, fellow administrators, and others who are necessary to alleviate the problems that have been brought to her attention. It may be difficult for the Affirmative Action Officer to guarantee confidentiality while seeking to effect changes in particular cases, due both to the dependence of her office on other offices on campus and to the fact that cooperation with the Affirmative Action Officer is not required of the administrators, faculty, or staff of the college.

The Ombudsperson. In addition to these offices, many colleges have an Office of the Ombudsperson, although the office may be known by different names at different schools. This office does not fit into the protocol of the campus administration and so it can be approached at any time. The purpose of the campus Ombudsperson is to provide an internal mediator for students who are having a problem at the college. Any student can approach the Ombudsperson with the security of knowing that all conversations will be kept entirely confidential. The Ombudsperson, once approached by a student, will work with the student to remedy the problem at hand. While the Office of the Ombudsperson is officially a part of the Office of the President of the college, it is an independent office and the Ombudsperson does not report to anyone in the administration. This independent status within the Office of the President is what gives the Ombudsperson sufficient authority to solve students' problems. The Ombudsperson also has access to all files on campus, unless they are protected by law. This access is useful and, in some cases, essential.

The Office of the Ombudsperson is an excellent resource if you have been denied access to a course or if you have been denied some academic award or benefit as a result of sex discrimination. The Ombudsperson not only can investigate whether the professor or professors involved have exhibited a pattern of discriminatory behavior, but can also negotiate fair treatment for you. Similarly, if you have reason to believe that the placement service is inappropriately denying you access to certain student employment, then the Office of the Ombudsperson may be an excellent place to go. If you are already working on campus and your salary is not on a par with the salaries of other people holding comparable jobs, then the Ombudsperson should be able to intervene and have the inequity corrected.

In situations in which you cannot participate at all, or cannot participate to the extent that men at college can, in a particular club or in a specific sport, you can take this up as well with the Ombudsperson. The situation may call for no more than the Ombudsperson to make certain confidential inquiries and to inform the relevant people of the campus's obligation to provide equal opportunity.

If for some reason your problem cannot be handled by this office, the Ombudsperson can direct you to the appropriate person or office on your campus who can.

Campus Grievance Committees and Procedures. Different offices of the university may have established grievance procedures for students to follow. The Office of Student Employment, for instance, should have a set of procedures for you to follow if you suspect any employment discrimination against you. These procedures will specify how to file a complaint and which campus committees or offices will take up the complaint should you fail to receive adequate resolution at any particular stage.

All universities are now required by law to have grievance procedures for students to follow for sexual harassment and sex discrimination. A grievance committee is usually formed from members of the staff and faculty of the college. The committee members might be elected, but more often they are volunteers or are appointed through their departments or by a dean. Part of the task set for such committees is to formulate a grievance procedure for students to follow. Your campus may even have a special committee designated specifically to deal with sex discrimination complaints. There may be a special subcommittee of the general committee to handle these complaints. It is also likely that special committee members have been trained or briefed in issues, procedures, and solutions relevant to sex discrimination. Generally the complaints filed by students to the grievance committee are heard and retained on a confidential basis. In general, grievance committees will keep their own files. Solutions are sought in such a manner that this confidentiality need not be breeched. But for some sorts of discrimination problems, in order to work toward a solution the source must be revealed. In such cases, the committee ought to leave the decision up to the student whether the committee should pursue the matter further. Sometimes grievance procedures and committees are formed with the cooperation of the Affirmative Action Officer. However, once formed, the committees should operate independently from the Office of Affirmative Action.

You may want to approach the Affirmative Action Office, or the Office of the Ombudsperson, in order to find out about existing grievance procedures and committees on your campus. Other sources of information about grievance procedures and committees are the Office of Public Information and the Office of the Secretary of the College. Bear in mind that any one office on campus may not be informed about all of the procedures and committees established at your college. It is possible, for instance, that the person you speak with in the dean's office will not know about the grievance procedures that have been set up in the work-study office.

When to Bypass Protocol
Remember that in approaching administrators, it is important to follow protocol in the campus hierarchy. There are at least two exceptions to this rule, however. The first exception applies also to treating problems as instances of the stacked-deck effect. You are in an exceptional situation of this first sort if, for whatever reasons, you feel that you cannot discuss the problem you are having with the relevant person. Suppose, for example, that Quintana's supervisor is also the Chair of Quintana's major department, and that Quintana is con-

vinced that this person would look highly unfavorably upon any complaint that she lodged. If Quintana has reason to believe that her attempts to handle the problem as the stacked-deck effect will meet with hostility from someone whose benevolence she feels she depends on, then she may proceed directly to the steps discussed in this section.

Hostility toward those who attempt to address some form of the stacked-deck effect is in and of itself a contribution to discrimination. If Quintana has reason to believe that someone in a particular office will be hostile to her approaches, then she may legitimately choose to circumvent that office. This might be the case, for example, if a friend of Quintana's had already encountered difficulties with the people in that office. If you have encountered either the stacked-deck effect or sex discrimination and you have good reason to believe that following campus protocol will lead you to an unreceptive or hostile audience, then you should proceed to the next level of intervention.

The second exception has already been mentioned. If you simply want to bring a problem to the attention of the administration, and are not seeking a specific remedy to the problem, then it is also acceptable to bypass protocol. Since it is the business of the Affirmative Action Officer to keep records of discrimination on campus and to monitor the college's remedial action, you should certainly discuss your concerns with her. Because communication between administrative offices is never perfect, however, you may feel that this is not enough. It might also be useful to inform the Dean of Student Affairs of the problem as well as the Ombudsperson, if there is one on your campus. Both of these people come into contact with many students and your comments will make it possible for them to begin to discern a pattern of related problems in other students' experiences, if one exists.

General Strategy
There are some general points you should keep in mind while you are contemplating your approach to a problem of discrimination on your campus. After you have formulated a statement of the problem, you should ask yourself whether your problem is the problem of an individual or of a group. In a way, any problem of sex discrimination is the problem of women as a group. But in some instances, only a particular woman may be affected directly. To return to Quintana, unless there are other women working in her office under inequitable salary conditions, the immediate problem that Quintana faces is hers alone. Quintana's may be a case of an individual facing sex discrimination.

On the other hand, a woman's sport that is given inequitable facilities presents an immediate problem to a group of women. Another sort of problem for which a group of women might want to
approach the administration together would be a situation in which
each of you had individually experienced a similar difficulty. A good
example of this comes up frequently in cases of sexual harassment.
If you are being harassed by a professor, it is quite likely that other
women students have also been harassed by the same professor.
With a little effort you might be able to locate these women. If
the problem you are confronted with is indeed a group problem,
then it might be easier and more forceful if some or all of you
go together to approach the appropriate campus office about the
problem.

Before you approach a campus official with your problem, you
must carefully go over all of the evidence you have in support of
your assertions. It would be useful to write down all the pieces of
evidence that you have, including detailed notes on or transcriptions
of relevant conversations, complete with participants' names and
dates of their occurrence. Evidence of discrimination may take many
forms. It might, for instance, come in the form of explicit remarks
made to you by professors who were involved in the discriminatory
act or decision. It might take the form of a decision criterion that
has disproportionate impact on you as a woman. It might take the
form of a pattern of discriminatory behavior; for example, if a department with a large proportion of majors who are women awards
no or very few teaching assistantships to female students, this is
clear evidence of a problem. The evidence might also take the form
of an omission, for example, if you ask to be referred for a research
position and the employment office refuses to refer you or to give
you an explanation for their failure to act.

Because these problems are so varied, what will count as evidence
of them will vary accordingly. It is important to keep in mind that
you do not need proof of sex discrimination in order to approach the
administration. In some cases, a mere hunch on your part may be
sufficient. But you will need to convince whichever administrator
you talk to that, at the least, your problem may be the *result* of sex
discrimination. Unless you have some evidence by means of which
you can convince someone of this, then there will be no reason for
the administration to investigate your problem. How strong your
evidence must be depends very much on the particulars of the problem. In some cases, a well-articulated hunch will be enough to com-
pel an administrator to look into the matter. In other cases, something
more will be required. The stronger your evidence is, however, the

better your chances of achieving results by approaching the administration.

For this reason, it is a good idea to keep a record of facts and events relating to your problem as they occur. *As soon as you begin to suspect that you may have a problem, start keeping accurate and explicit notes on any and all pertinent incidents. Include names, dates, and verbatim quotations where possible.* These notes will give you invaluable perspective on the problem; they will assist you in presenting your problem to others; and, should legal action ever become necessary, they will prove vital to your case.

Another thing to think about before you approach the administration is how to present your problem. You have a description of the problem, a list of your evidence for it, and you may have some ideas about possible remedies. Now what you need to think about is how to discuss the matter in a way that increases the likelihood of the most productive outcome. One important strategy to keep in mind is that in many cases it is best to avoid a conflict situation that will divide people into "sides," such as a student against faculty or administration, women against men, or any other such opposition. You should be assertive and persistent, but you should allow room for the person you're speaking with to sympathize with what you're saying. Thus, you should avoid discussing the problem in stark terms unless this is truly called for. In discussing remedies to the problem you should not start by making absolute demands. Rather, give the person you are talking to an opportunity to alleviate or eradicate the problem.

When the behavior of campus officials serves to deprive you of equal educational or employment opportunities on the basis of your gender, that behavior is more than likely illegal. If you have reason to believe that you have been discriminated against, then legal action may be appropriate. However, in the overwhelming majority of cases of discrimination involving undergraduates, legal action is either impossible, ineffective, or otherwise inappropriate. That is why this book has focused on the many avenues already available to women students to help them overcome sex discrimination in college. If these means fail, read on to Get Smart Course 505 for a discussion of your legal rights as a woman in college. Whether or not you ever intend to use the legal system, you should be aware of your legal rights.

Rape Prevention and Intervention
The prevention of rape on campus is the concern not only of every woman on campus but of the college administration as well. In fact, a good deal of the responsibility for your safety on campus lies with

the administration. Thus, if your campus presents any unsafe situations—dark paths, unguarded buildings, inadequate security for classes given at odd hours, to name a few—this is not a fact of college life that you must accept. Speak up; bring the problem to the attention of the administration according to the channels outlined earlier in this chapter. The college should provide you with as safe a campus environment as possible.

It might be that your campus already has a rape prevention program. If not, there may be one in the nearby vicinity of your campus. Rape prevention programs initiated on college campuses can include safety evaluation techniques, increased security measures, escort services to and from campus buildings and activities, automobile escort services for longer distances, training sessions for personal safety, consciousness-raising groups on the problem of rape, and information dissemination in the form of booklets, pamphlets, and films, as well as follow-up medical and counseling services. Consult your local Women's Center or the Student Health Service. If your college doesn't have adequate prevention and follow-up services and you are interested in seeing such services set up, then it may be useful to approach the director of the college health service directly, since such programs would generally be run under the auspices of the student health service.

You might want to make yourself familiar with the rape prevention and intervention programs nearest you. Many hospital emergency rooms now have rape crisis intervention programs. There may be a sexual assault hot line in your area that can provide information on the nearest program. If not, the local police station should have that information. You could participate in the ongoing activities of such a program, attend classes in personal safety or self-defense, or do volunteer work.

Above all, in uncomfortable, threatening, or dangerous situations you should trust your instincts. Learn to say no loudly and clearly when this is how you feel, learn to remove yourself immediately from situations in which you sense a threat, and, in general, trust your own perception of potential danger.

If you are raped, you should go immediately to the nearest rape crisis center, the emergency room of the local hospital, or the Student Health Service, and you should call the police. A crime has been committed, and the sooner the police are informed, the sooner the criminal can be apprehended. In addition, the police should be able to locate a hospital with adequate facilities for you, if you have not already done so. Calling the police does not mean that you must prosecute. But even if you are unsure of whether to press charges, allowing the health service or hospital to provide medical evidence and reporting the crime immediately to the police will make it easier for the case to be prosecuted should you decide to press charges at a later date.

Solutions Summary

- The first thing to do when you encounter a gender-related problem on your campus is to follow the advice in the "Solutions" sections of Get Smart Courses 101, 202, and 303 to make sure that you have already tried all the relevant techniques for your problem described there.
- Construct a clear statement or description of your problem. If possible, find other women who share the problem and tackle it together. Amass and check the accuracy of your evidence; keep as detailed notes on the problem as possible. Think about what sorts of solutions are relevant and appropriate to your problem.
- Become familiar with the hierarchy of campus offices to go to for help, including these key administrative posts:
  The Ombudsperson. The Ombudsperson serves as a mediator for all students. The Ombudsperson hears grievances and problems on a confidential basis and is an independent organ of the Office of the President.
  The Dean of Students. This dean is available to meet with students and handles student affairs on campus, from course offerings to social activities. Be aware that problems brought to the dean might not be treated confidentially.
  The Office of Affirmative Action. Every institution of higher education that receives federal funds must have an Office of Affirmative Action and make its campus address and phone number available to all students, faculty, and staff. The Affirmative Action Officer hears complaints of harassment and discrimination, keeps accurate files of such complaints and subsequent investigations, and protects the institution from legal and other action filed against it on the grounds of harassment and discrimination.
  Special Grievance Committees. Your college should have special procedures, panels, or committees to hear, review, and investigate complaints of sexual harassment or discrimination. The Affirmative Action Officer should be able to direct you to them.
- Familiarize yourself with the programs available on your campus or in your local community concerning violence against women on campus.

Get Smart
Course 505

The Law:
Know Your Legal Rights
and Remedies

Sex discrimination, including sexual harassment, is now against the law in virtually all institutions of higher education. It is important for you to be aware of your legal rights as a student.

It is rarely necessary, productive, or even possible for an individual undergraduate to sue a college for sex discrimination. Nevertheless, cases arise for which legal action should be considered, for instance, when the campus administration fails to redress adequately a problem of sex discrimination.

This chapter will introduce you to relevant civil rights legislation and discuss the possibilities and pitfalls of legal action for the student.

This chapter explains key legal tools currently used to fight sex discrimination in higher education. These tools consist primarily of Title VII of the Civil Rights Act of 1964 and Title IX of the Education Amendments of 1972. The purpose of this discussion is to familiarize you with the basic legal rights of college students and campus employees. In addition, we will apprise you of some of the pitfalls of legal recourse. In contemplating legal action, it is important to consider both the pros and cons with care. We urge you to try the other remedies we've suggested in the preceding chapters first. But whatever you do, you should know your rights.

There are several benefits to knowing where you stand legally. In the first place, it may be immediately useful to know the facts of your entitlements. For example, consider how Therese makes use of her knowledge of the law. Therese is experiencing sex discrimination in the accounting department, where she is studying to be a certified public accountant. She has exhausted other remedies, and now goes to talk to the Dean of Students, Dean Trump. Unfortunately for Therese, this dean is not sympathetic to her problem, and tells her:

"I can see that you are upset, but you have to realize how much progress we've made. The college is making a good faith effort to be sensitive to women: we have a committee on sex discrimination, a committee investigating the inclusion of more women in the curriculum, and a faculty of sincere, good-hearted men and women who are genuinely concerned with the problem. We have even set up an Office of Affirmative Action to handle serious problems if they come up. This shows how seriously we take the problem. Therese, your situation is simply not a case for that office. By complaining, you are just going to upset the professors involved, and make things harder for yourself. To speak to the Affirmative Action Officer now would be counterproductive."

Therese knows that the existence of the Office of Affirmative Action is mandated by federal law: it is *not* a special favor that the administration has tendered to the women on campus. And she immediately sees the peculiarity of Dean Trump's argument. The purpose of such an office should be to facilitate, rather than block, a student's attempt to get help with such problems.

The second advantage to knowing your rights under the law is that it can help make you a more effective activist, even in cases where you do not intend to go to court. If Therese knows that the accounting department's treatment of her has violated the law, she can have a ready response to the dean's remarks:

"I appreciate how much the administration has already accomplished, and that's why I've come to you to discuss this problem. I have tried working things out with the individual professors involved, but I haven't gotten anywhere. On the other hand, the department's policy is clearly in violation of Title IX legislation. As I see it, you and I are on the same side: we both want to resolve this problem as quickly and with as little trouble as possible. I'm hoping that you will help me with this."

Dean Trump certainly has an interest in protecting the college from embarrassing and costly legal action. It is quite possible that the dean was unaware that the complaint in question involved a violation of the law. Therese's answer alerts Dean Trump to the seriousness of the problem from the administration's point of view: the dean cannot afford to overlook a violation of the law so long as Therese is clearly not going to drop the matter. But at the same time, Therese addresses Dean Trump as an ally, not an adversary, and enlists the dean's assistance in solving a common problem.

Therese's knowledge of the law enables her to impress Dean Trump with the idea that she will not let the situation remain as it is, and that the dean must take the complaint seriously. This is so even though Therese does not wish to have to take the matter into a court of law.

Finally, knowing your rights will enable you to recognize situations in which legal recourse becomes appropriate. The law on sex discrimination and sexual harassment is complex and constantly evolving. In addition, your specific protection under the law will depend on the type of college you attend, since students have different rights at different kinds of colleges. And there are differences in the courts' behavior from state to state. This chapter will not tell you all there is to know by any means. But the basic overview of the law that it provides will help you distinguish problems that the law may address. This will help you decide when you might benefit from consulting with a lawyer or other expert and when legal action might be called for.

Basic Legislation

There are two pieces of legislation of particular relevance to the rights of women in college. The first is Title IX of the Education Amendments of 1972, which went into effect in July 1975. The second is Title VII of the Civil Rights Act of 1964 with its subsequent amendments. Title VII applies specifically to employment, and is relevant to students who are also employees of the college.

Title IX of the Education Amendments prohibits discrimination against students and employees on the basis of sex. It covers all colleges that receive federal funds in the form of grants, loans, and contracts. Three kinds of institutions are exempt from this law: religious institutions, when the anti-discrimination provision is inconsistent with their religious tenets; military institutions, when their primary purpose is to train individuals for the military services of the United States or the Merchant Marine; and private undergraduate and single-sex public undergraduate institutions, but *only* with respect to admissions.

Title IX was written to prohibit discrimination on the basis of sex in all aspects of education. The law states:

> No person shall, on the basis of sex, be excluded from the participation in, be denied the benefits of, or be subjected to discrimination under any education program or activity receiving federal financial assistance.

Title IX coverage includes the disparate impact of a college's policies and practices, graduation requirements, housing, facilities, access to course offerings, counseling, financial assistance, athletic programs and scholarships, medical services and insurance, student employment and general employment, and salaries and benefits.

The law does not specifically require that women and men be treated identically, but rather that everyone, regardless of sex, be given equal opportunity. This means, for example, that it is permissible under Title IX for a college to maintain single-sex sports teams, as long as all students have equal opportunity to play the sports of their choice. Under Title IX a college is also not required to have the same number of women's sports teams as men's sports teams. However, there must be sufficient women's teams at the college to meet the interests of the women students to the same degree that the men students' interests are met. In similar fashion, women must, under Title IX, be provided with university housing in the same proportion and at similar quality as are the men. And the same reasoning applies to the other campus activities, facilities, and programs.

Title VII of the Civil Rights Act in its current form prohibits discrimination in employment on the basis of five categories, one of which is sex. All aspects of employment are covered, including hiring, upgrading, salaries, fringe benefits, training, and treatment of pregnancy and related conditions. All employees are protected under Title VII, including students who are also employees of their colleges. Every college with over fifteen employees is covered with respect to sex discrimination, with the exception of religious institutions.

Sexual harassment of employees is clearly included as a violation of Title VII. In November 1980, the federal office responsible for the enforcement of Title VII issued guidelines for interpreting the coverage of sexual harassment under the law. The guidelines state that

> unwelcome sexual advances, requests for sexual favors, and other verbal or physical conduct of a sexual nature constitute sexual harassment when
> 1) submission to such conduct is made either explicitly or implicitly a term or condition of an individual's employment;
> 2) submission to or rejection of such conduct by an individual is used as the basis for employment decisions affecting such individual; or
> 3) such conduct has the purpose or effect of unreasonably interfering with an individual's work performance or creating an intimidating, hostile, or offensive working environment.

The guidelines further state that institutions should take preventive measures against sexual harassment, such as raising the subject of sexual harassment among the staff; expressing strong disapproval of sexual harassment; developing and implementing appropriate sanctions for harassment, as well as methods for educating all concerned about sexual harassment; and, finally, informing all employees of their rights under Title VII.

One further piece of legislation should be mentioned here, and that is the Age Discrimination Act of 1975, which prohibits discrimination on the basis of age in programs or activities receiving federal funds. This Act went into effect in January 1979, and is enforced by the federal Department of Education. A woman's age is often considered to be more significant than a man's age in college admissions, financial aid decisions, counseling, career planning, placement, health facilities, and athletics. This Act makes some progress toward protecting against age discrimination directed at women in college.

Interpretation and Coverage
The specific protections afforded students by the law are affected by several factors. As we mentioned, federal civil rights laws apply differently to different types of institutions. States may also have their

own legislation, and state coverage depends on where your college is located. In addition, your college may issue its own internal guidelines for the interpretation of sexual harassment and procedures for addressing problems of discrimination. Finally, courts of law *interpret* legislation, and their interpretations influence future court decisions. This means that the kind of action that a court can take also varies from state to state, and changes as new decisions are made.

In April 1983, Dean Henry Rosovsky of Harvard University circulated a letter to all students, staff, and faculty, which reported the findings of the Faculty Council of Harvard University concerning sexual harassment. In the letter, Dean Rosovsky formulated the working definition of sexual harassment that Harvard would observe:

> In the academic context, the term "sexual harassment" may be used to describe a wide range of behavior. The fundamental element is that inappropriate personal attention by an instructor or other officer who is in a position to determine a student's grade or otherwise affect the student's academic performance or professional future. Such behavior is unacceptable in a university because it is a form of unprofessional behavior which seriously undermines the atmosphere of trust essential to the academic enterprise.

This definition of sexual harassment is extremely broad, covering even the subtlest situations. Harvard's grievance procedures therefore supply students with internal recourse in a wide variety of problematic situations, independently of how the courts might construe sexual harassment.

Your university may also have an official policy on sexual harassment. If not, you may want to work toward developing one. A clear and broad definition of sexual harassment, and a strong policy against it, may better protect students while eliminating the need to seek redress in the courts. The courts have also sometimes interpreted sexual harassment broadly, but there is no universal legal definition.

There is one court decision that has restricted the coverage of Title IX in such a fundamental way that we discuss it here. This is the *Grove City College v. Bell, Secretary of Education* case, which was decided in 1984. The *Grove City College* decision narrowed the scope of Title IX to include only the specific part of a college that receives direct federal funding, rather than the entire institution. This meant, for example, that if an incident of sexual harassment occurred in a building that was not specifically built or renovated with federal funds, the incident could not be investigated as a potential violation of Title IX. Because 96 percent of the federal funds that go to educational institutions and programs are not earmarked for specific programs, the effect of the *Grove City* decision is far-reaching. In the fourteen months following the decision, the Office for Civil Rights closed, limited, or suspended sixty-three discrimination cases.

The *Grove City* ruling was an unfortunate turn of events for the enforcement of nondiscrimination and the Title IX regulation. A bill designed to overturn the decision—the Civil Rights Restoration Act of 1985—was introduced into the House of Representatives on January 24, 1985, and the Senate on February 7, 1985. By March 1988, the Senate and the House had passed it. However, an amendment was attached to the bill stipulating that institutions receiving federal funds were not required to provide or pay for abortions. The intention of this amendment is to prevent charges of discrimination based on failure to offer abortion or related services.

Legal Recourse

It is one thing to know when injustice is being done. It is another to know when your rights are being violated according to the letter of the law, and yet another to decide when your rights are being violated according to the spirit of the law. But beyond well-documented and blatant cases of sexual harassment or sex discrimination, knowing how the courts in your state are likely to interpret and implement the law is something else again. There is no substitute in this matter for consultations with experts, or for simply handing matters over to the appropriate agencies.

Various legal resources are available to students short of hiring private lawyers. Campus offices that may be of assistance are discussed in the "Solutions" section of Get Smart 404. In addition, your college may have a student union that employs lawyers for the students. A local feminist law center, or public interest law firm, may also be available to provide assistance. Students also have direct recourse to the government offices responsible for the implementation of Title IX and Title VII legislation.

Title IX is enforced by the federal government's Office for Civil Rights in the Department of Education. The Office for Civil Rights (commonly known as the OCR) has regional and local offices around the country, and if you think you have been discriminated against or harassed under the terms of Title IX, it is worthwhile contacting your local branch of the OCR for information concerning procedures for filing complaints.

In general, complaints of violations of Title IX can be made by individuals by writing a letter to the Secretary of the Department of Education or to the OCR directly. The time limit for filing a complaint is 180 days from the last act of discrimination covered in the complaint. However, the Department of Education can extend this time limit if good cause is demonstrated.

An organization can also file a complaint on behalf of an individual, as well as on behalf of a class, or group, of people. An organization can also file a complaint concerning a pattern of discriminatory behavior without identifying specific individuals.

When a complaint is filed with the OCR, it notifies the college mentioned in the complaint within fifteen days. If voluntary compliance with Title IX fails at the college, the OCR can begin proceedings to suspend or terminate the federal funds the school is receiving. The OCR is also empowered to bar future awards of funds to the college, and it may recommend court action.

When the OCR investigates a complaint, the people involved in the case are not bound by a confidentiality requirement. This means that the identities of individuals involved in filing the complaint may be revealed in the course of an investigation. At the same time, institutions must keep and preserve specified records relevant to the determination of whether violations of Title IX have occurred. The OCR has the power to review all such records.

Colleges are required under Title IX to designate at least one employee responsible for coordinating the institutions' efforts to comply with Title IX. This may be the Affirmative Action Officer, but the title of the officer varies from campus to campus and is sometimes simply called the Title IX Officer. Sometimes an administrator, for instance, a dean, performs the Title IX Officer's duties, without having the specific title for this responsibility.

The employee designated in compliance with Title IX is responsible for investigating all Title IX complaints. The college must also notify all students and employees of the appointment of the Title IX Officer, and supply the officer's name, office address, and telephone number.

Title IX also requires that each college covered under the regulation adopt grievance procedures for its students and staff, although no specific procedures are required. Each college is responsible for publishing an explanation of its grievance procedures and must distribute it to the students and staff. Students are not required to use the grievance procedures, and may complain directly to the OCR at any time.

Colleges are prohibited from discharging or discriminating against any participant or potential participant in a complaint on the basis of her having made the complaint, assisted with an investigation of a complaint, or instituted proceedings to redress a complaint. Violating this prohibition is known as *retaliation* and is a serious problem, since it provides strong incentive against lodging complaints and additionally punishes those who have already been harassed or discriminated against. *It is important to know that you are legally protected from retaliation.* In some cases, even where the grounds for the original complaint are unclear, subsequent retaliation on the part of university staff or administration may itself supply clear grounds for the OCR and other legal action.

Title VII is also enforced by the federal government, specifically by the Equal Employment Opportunity Commission (EEOC). Like the OCR, the EEOC has local branches that can be contacted directly.

The EEOC cannot undertake any investigation without a filed complaint, which must be made on their complaint form. Those who are permitted to file a complaint are the aggrieved employee or employees, aggrieved job applicant or applicants, as well as any individual or organization complaining on behalf of the aggrieved, and, finally, members of the EEOC itself. The time limit for filing a complaint is 180 days from the last act of discrimination mentioned in the complaint. Complaints can be filed on behalf of a class of grievants or concerning a pattern of discriminatory behavior, without identifying individuals.

Once a complaint has been filed with the EEOC under Title VII, the EEOC notifies the institution involved within ten days and conducts an investigation. The charges are not made public by the EEOC, nor can any of its efforts during the conciliation process be made public by the EEOC. The people involved in the case are not bound by a confidentiality requirement, however, and, if court action becomes necessary, the identity of all parties involved becomes a matter of public record, as is the case in all court actions. If no resolution is found, either the EEOC or the U. S. Attorney General may file suit, though neither is required to do so. The EEOC files suit in cases involving private institutions, and the Attorney General files in cases involving public institutions.

After being investigated by the EEOC, a college must keep and preserve records relevant to the determination of whether or not violations have occurred. The government is empowered to review all of these records. As in the case of complaints filed with the OCR, colleges are prohibited from engaging in retaliation against those involved in making the complaint.

Private Legal Action

In any matter that the OCR or the EEOC is empowered to investigate, individuals may initiate their own lawsuits as well. Court actions can include awarding equitable relief and back pay to employees or requiring that the college cease its unlawful behavior, institute appropriate affirmative action, and reinstate employees. In some cases, civil suits are also possible.

When considering legal action, it is important to bear in mind that state laws may be applicable. You can check with the Attorney General in the state where you go to school, the state Civil Rights Commission, or the state Women's Commission, which is usually located in the state capitol, to see which state anti-discrimination laws cover your college. In cases of sexual harassment, state laws concerning sexual abuse and assault may also be applicable.

The most important initial step that you can take when you are contemplating legal action is to obtain good, solid advice and to try to find a lawyer with whom you will be able to work on a long-term basis. It is important that the lawyers you consult be experts in the field of discrimination law, preferably with experience in higher education discrimination law, since the law is a complicated matter and the lawyer needs to have detailed knowledge of specific courts and precedents. It is a good idea to consult with several people— perhaps someone from a local feminist law center, and one or two private lawyers if possible, in order to get some feel for the vagaries of your case and the different possible approaches.

There are several things you need to find out. The first is whether you have a viable court case in the first place, and what possible outcomes a court proceeding might have. It may be that even though you have been clearly discriminated against, your particular case or the circumstances surrounding it, together with the behavior of the courts in your jurisdiction, may render success in court unlikely. On the other hand, a lawyer may see an alternative route to a lawsuit than the one you had in mind originally.

It may also be that, even though you have a strong case, winning it would not provide you with satisfactory compensation. You need to hear some expert opinion on what you might hope to achieve by winning a case, and to decide whether such an outcome would be worth the costs—financial and other—of a suit.

You also need to find out about the cost of legal action. You may be able to find a lawyer willing to work on a contingency basis. If not, a court case can be exorbitantly expensive. One reason for the high cost of legal action is the amount of time it requires. Legal recourse is a very slow process. A lawsuit can take years to complete; it can span as much as a decade. Once you have initiated a suit, though, your college might offer to settle with you out of court in exchange for your dropping the suit. Such settlements may be preferable on both sides: remedies may be implemented and individuals may be paid damages or back pay; the time, trouble, and expense of legal action is saved by both sides; and, if it would have been found guilty of the charges, the college avoids the risk of more severe sanctions against it—sanctions that could include the withdrawal of federal funds awarded to the college, both present and future.

Recently, colleges have begun taking out insurance to protect themselves against sexual harassment and discrimination suits. And some institutions prefer to litigate to the very end rather than settle a case. A university generally has far more resources to sustain it through a long suit than does an individual, and time and money alone can win the case for the college in the end.

When calculating the costs of a lawsuit, you should also be aware of the fact that legal action makes you very unpopular. It may seem obvious that individuals charged in a civil rights action might become hostile toward you, and even that other faculty and administrators would take sides against you. But it is hard to imagine beforehand the extent of the hostility that you may encounter. Sadly, much of it may come from those you count as allies; whenever the boat gets rocked, people become nervous, and the people in the most precarious positions feel the most threatened of all. When a student files sex discrimination or sexual harassment charges, other students are made to feel the threat against the status quo as dangerous to themselves, and they may hold the student who complains—rather than the institution that discriminates—responsible for her own situation.

For all of these reasons, a class action suit may be preferable to an individual suit. The impact of a class action suit on the university may also be greater. If you have any reason to believe that the problem you are having may be a problem others are having as well—as is usually the case—you should look into the possibility of bringing a suit as a group.

It is important to be aware of the various costs and limited benefits to be derived for the individual who sues. There is no substitute for sound legal advice. And before you do anything, we strongly urge you to go back through the "Solutions" sections of the previous chapters. Be sure that you have already tried the relevant remedies available on your campus. Moreover, do not neglect the advice from Get Smart Course 404 on keeping a written record of your problem as it develops.

The law is a valuable instrument of social change, and individual civil suits, along with class action suits, constitute important vehicles for change. When the policies of your college, or the actions of officials of the college, constitute violations of your rights, then a lawsuit is justified. It may be your best recourse and, in any case, is bound ultimately to benefit future generations of women in college.

Commencement

From Coed to Coeval:
College Truly Is a
Woman's Place

Women now make up more than half of the country's university students: The college campus is truly a woman's place. "That's all very fine and good," you may be saying to yourself, "but then, how come everything on campus conspires to make things harder for me just because I'm a woman?" This Commencement Exercise will try to answer that question.

In a certain sense everything in this book has been about *tracking systems*. Get Smart Course 404 is most obviously about tracking systems, since it talks about ways in which university policies track or guide women in different directions than men. Get Smart Course 303 is also about tracking systems: it shows how decision-making procedures can track women and men in different directions. But Courses 101 and 202 are also about tracking systems, since they discuss many aspects of social interaction that both facilitate and perpetuate procedural and policy tracking systems in the university. These tracking systems are integrally related. But why are you being "tracked" at all in college?

To answer this question, let's look at a hypothetical university—we'll call it Composite University. Composite University is an imaginary college based on national statistics on enrollment and employment, and on some details of individual universities.* Composite University is a complex, large social system. Within this system, women find themselves concentrated in certain roles and positions, while men find themselves concentrated in others. By looking at the social structure of Composite University, we'll be able to learn a great deal about how and why the tracking system operates at the undergraduate level.

Composite University

The total student population of Composite University is 20,000. This includes undergraduates, graduate students, and students attending the university's professional schools. This makes Composite University the size of a large private university, or a middle-sized public university. The student population has been chosen for convenience—looking at a large university will show some things more clearly, but the basic composition of Composite U. will hold for smaller colleges too. How closely your campus resembles Composite

*National statistics are based on the *Digest of Education Statistics 1987* (Washington, D.C.: Center for Education Statistics); "Becoming a Priority: The Status of University and College Office Staff," National Association of Office Workers, March 1980; *On Campus with Women* 14, no. 1 (Summer 1984) and no. 4 (Spring 1985).

University will depend on a number of factors: the size of the school; whether the university is private or public; whether the university is coeducational and, if so, how long it has been; whether your college is two- or four-year and whether there are graduate or professional schools affiliated with it; and all of the idiosyncrasies of the college administration. In its essentials, Composite University is a pretty good approximation of many universities.

The university work force can be divided into several categories. For our purposes, we've divided the work force of Composite University into six job categories, indicating the proportion of the total work force each category represents:

1. Faculty and research staff (38%)
2. Professional library staff (2%)
3. Clerical and secretarial staff (27.5%)
4. Service and maintenance staff (13.5%)
5. Craftspeople, including mechanics and other skilled workers (9.6%)
6. Administration, excluding professors who also hold administrative positions such as department Chair (9.4%)

So the largest single category of Composite University's work force is faculty and research staff (38%). Of the remaining 62 percent, roughly half are clerical and secretarial staff and half are all other campus workers.

Women are not represented in equal proportions in each of these categories at Composite University. Table 1 shows the number of employees in each category, and the number and percentage of those employees who are women.

The table shows that the percentage of women service and maintenance workers at Composite University is not very high (19.1%). On the other hand, the percentage of women clerical and secretarial workers is quite high (72.9%). Women at Composite University tend to be concentrated in certain areas of employment.

As might be expected, there is no shortage of women on the campus of Composite University. The student body of 20,000 follows the national average in being composed of 52.5 percent women. This means that all together, students and employees combined, 49.9 percent of the people on campus are women. That makes Composite University pretty close to average.

Table 1 really gives only a broad overview of the composition of the work force at Composite University. Within each job category there are a number of different positions. A closer look at each cat-

Table 1. Proportion of Women Employees at Composite University

	Total Employees	Women Employees	Women Employees (as a % of total)
Faculty & research staff	2,533	775	30.6
Professional library staff	133	80	60.0
Clerical & secretarial staff	1,833	1,336	72.9
Service & maintenance staff	900	172	19.1
Craftspeople	640	175	27.3
Administration	627	290	46.3
Total Employed	6,666	2,828	42%

egory shows that women and men are clustered in certain areas. For example, the category of clerical and secretarial workers includes supervisors and certain kinds of clerks, 16.7 percent of whom are women. The majority of workers in this category are secretaries, however, and 90 percent of the secretaries at Composite University are women.

A similar pattern can be seen in the category of service and maintenance staff. Only 19.1 percent of these employees are women. But this includes both full-time and part-time workers. Of the full-time workers in this category, only 16.3 percent are women; of the part-time workers, 75 percent are women. Service and maintenance employees include janitors and cleaners, 90 percent of whom are women at Composite University. It also includes food preparation workers, of whom women make up 93.8 percent. Interestingly, of the fifteen cooks at Composite University, not one of them is a woman.

In every job category, similar male/female clusters can be found. In the category of skilled crafts, there are no women mechanics at Composite University, out of a total of 125 people with that rank. On the other hand, women make up 77.8 percent of reporters, editors, and technicians.

While 27 percent of all full-time faculty at Composite University are women, only 11 percent of all full professors are women; 22 percent of all associate professors are women; 35 percent of all assistant professors are women; 43 percent of all instructors are women; and 45 percent of all lecturers are women. In addition, at Composite University, women account for more than half of the part-time adjuncts. These are people who are generally employed for only a semester or two.

Women also tend to be clustered in certain areas of employment within the library and administration categories. Only 22.5 percent of upper-level administrators at Composite University are women. The university has never had a woman president.

Incidentally, the kind of problem that Quintana faced in Get Smart Course 303—namely, receiving a lower wage than her male office mate—is not unusual on the university campus. At Composite University, women are clustered at job ranks with relatively low salaries. The average full professor (11 percent women) earns around $42,000, while the average secretary (90 percent women) earns around $15,000. In addition, at Composite University, women earn on the average 17 percent less than male colleagues who perform exactly the same work under exactly the same job description and title.

Implications for Undergraduates at Composite University

We've gotten a fairly good overview of the composition of the work force at Composite University. Let's consider what implications this has for the undergraduate attending Composite University.

Many of the men employed on campus are working in jobs that require little or no interaction with the undergraduate population. Engineers, air-conditioning repair persons, cooks, and high-ranking administrators seldom come in contact with students. On the other hand, secretaries, low-level administrators, and food preparation workers have frequent contact with students as a part of their daily routines.

The effect on the students of this job clustering by sex is to reinforce traditional ideas about what constitutes woman's work and men's work. But a little thought is all it takes to realize that man can also serve food, and women can also cook it.

Most of the faculty at Composite University are men, and this can certainly be a problem for the students. The fact that women tend to be clustered at lower-level faculty positions means that the turnover rate for women on the faculty is higher than it is for men. For the undergraduate trying to forge a long-term working relationship with a professor, it can be difficult to develop such a relationship with a female professor.

The makeup of the campus work force has certain other implications for the student, of which you should be aware. One concerns the concentration of authority in the upper reaches of administration. While even half or more of the total work force may be women, very few of those women have the authority to make policy decisions on a scale that affects students. Most of the people with this kind of authority on campus are men.

What this means is that a problem of particular concern to women on campus does not directly affect the people who fix policy. This does not mean that the men in these positions are incapable of understanding the problems women on campus may have, or that they are unwilling to take steps to improve matters. But it does mean it is to be expected that, until more women are appointed to high-level positions, substantive changes in areas of special importance to women on campus will be slow in coming.

To take one example, the Harvard study we cited in Orientation showed that 34 percent of women report having been sexually harassed at least once in the course of their undergraduate educations at Harvard University. The figure for men is 0 percent. Suppose it were the case that exactly 50 percent of the senior administrators at Composite University were women. If the Harvard figure were applied to Composite University, it would mean that 17 percent of the senior administrators would, in all probability, have themselves experienced sexual harassment as college students. Instead, because so few senior administrators at Composite University are women, it is much more likely that none of them ever experienced sexual harassment as an undergraduate. This does not mean that the administration cannot become sensitive to the issue and move to eliminate the problem. But it is clear that senior administration would move a lot more quickly if sexual harassment were a problem they themselves had had to face, and perhaps still faced, on a day-to-day basis.

Why Are You Being Tracked?
The university can be viewed as a large organism. The campus is its body. It has many different organs that perform different life-sustaining functions: there are different offices for different purposes; in each office, different people perform different jobs. The faculty instruct; the secretaries see to the necessary organizational and paperwork tasks that keep each organ running smoothly; the students study and pay tuition. Like any organism, this one is a creature of habit. It follows the same routines day in and day out. It breathes, eats, and sleeps regularly. The way things are now being done will

be the most comfortable way for the organism to get them done tomorrow.

It may seem to you at times that the university is a hostile place. But there's another way to view the matter, which probably comes somewhat closer to the truth. All the pressures you feel steering you in certain directions, whether by affecting the way you perceive yourself and think about your future or by placing certain obstacles in your path, are nothing more or less than the habits of a big, lazy organism trying to keep all of its organs working in the customary way.

Many people view the university as among the most liberal and progressive institutions in the United States. And it may seem strange to talk about it as a lazy, slow animal. But there are several reasons why the university organism is particularly lethargic when it comes to achieving substantive change for women.

In the first place, a great deal of evaluative decision making in universities is highly subjective. Decisions concerning the assignments of grades to papers, the awarding of Honors and academic prizes, the selection of students for research positions and postgraduate studies, and the hiring of faculty are frequently based on judgments made by individual professors concerning the merits of students and colleagues, judgments that rely on ill-defined criteria. It is very difficult to eliminate the influence of habits of thought and ingrained social biases on these kinds of decisions. This is one reason why decision making on university campuses tends to be conservative; it preserves the already existing social pattern rather than pressing for change.

Another reason for the slowness of the nation's universities in achieving equality for their female students has to do with the extent to which they are answerable to the law. While legislation from the 1960s to the present has given the courts the authority to intervene in sex discrimination in many areas, the courts have been extremely reluctant to enforce the existing legislation in dealing with university cases. One reason has been the unwillingness of the courts to decide cases involving judgments of academic quality. Such judgments are often at the fore of cases in which a university is sued for denying tenure on the basis of gender. Courts are reluctant to override the academic arguments for denial of tenure, on the grounds that they lack the relevant technical expertise—even though in other areas, such as medical malpractice cases, it has become routine practice for the courts to rely on expert testimony to make their decisions.

More recent developments in the interpretation of the law have further reduced the authority that the courts have to intervene in university cases. The most striking example of this was the *Grove City College* decision, discussed in Get Smart Course 505.

Another reason for the slowness of the universities to achieve sex equality has to do with the content of the college curriculum itself. The traditional liberal arts curriculum is made up almost entirely of the views of male thinkers on the subjects of Western culture. Some of these views are not conducive to enlightenment on the subject of equality of the sexes. In addition, the standard undergraduate curriculum frequently ignores or does not give credit to the contributions of female thinkers, not only on the subject of women but on any subject at all. Professors studied much the same curriculum when they were students. And in this way, a tradition of thought about women is passed on from generation to generation of college students. The fact is that, in spite of the obvious progress that has been made, college is not yet a place of equal educational opportunity for women. The weight of academic tradition is balanced against it.

The university tends to conserve energy by steering its inhabitants in certain directions. It tries to place people where it is most comfortable with them. A big, lazy animal is one you can get around, however. We've already taught you a lot about how to do this. Once you understand where it's pushing you, and are equipped with the intervention tools you've learned in this book, you can simply say "No! I'm going where I choose to go!" And with a little prodding from all of us, it won't be long until we've taught the whole creature to go where we need it to go.

While the universities have been slow to incorporate urgently needed reforms, progress has indeed been made. Now that you have read this book, you yourself know many ways in which you too can contribute much-needed impetus to the movement for equal educational opportunity for women in college. You are a part of the university organism, if only for a few years. Therefore, your awareness of the habits of the creature is already part of the process of waking it up. In addition, any action you undertake to resist the university's tracking system in your own case is a significant break with the creature's habits. And anything you do that has a concrete impact on those around you—whether it is a matter of pointing out something offensive to a professor, or of organizing women on your campus for some relevant purpose, or convincing the administration to change a discriminatory policy—is a real step forward for the whole body.

The authors of this book would appreciate hearing from you. If you have relevant comments or anecdotes regarding your college experiences, the application of interventions we have discussed in this book, or other interventions that you have found to be effective, please write to us:

Montana Katz and Veronica Vieland
The Feminist Press at the City University of New York
311 East 94 Street
New York, New York 10128

Appendix

Statistical Profile of Women in Higher Education in the United States

**Women as a percentage of students enrolled in
higher education in 1985**

All higher education	52.5%
Undergraduate	53.0%
Graduate	48.9%
Continuing education	65.1%
Part-time	57.3%

Source: Digest of Education Statistics 1987, tables 101, 103, 104, 217.

Minority women as a percentage of total enrollment in 1984

American Indian/Alaskan Native women	0.4%
Asian or Pacific Islander women	1.4%
Black women	5.2%
Hispanic women	2.3%

Source: Digest of Education Statistics 1987, table 131.

Minority women as a percentage of undergraduate students in 1984

American Indian/Alaskan Native women	0.4%
Asian or Pacific Islander women	1.5%
Black women	5.6%
Hispanic women	2.4%

Source: Digest of Education Statistics 1987, table 131.

Minority women as a percentage of total graduate students in 1984

American Indian/Alaskan Native women	0.18%
Asian or Pacific Islander women	0.9%
Black women	3.0%
Hispanic women	1.2%

Source: Digest of Education Statistics 1987, table 131.

Percentage of degrees received by women

	B.A.	M.A.	Ph.D.
1870	15	N.A.	0
1880	19	1	6
1890	17	19	1
1900	19	19	6
1910	23	26	10
1920	34	30	15
1930	40	40	15
1940	41	38	13
1950	24	29	10
1960	35	32	11
1970	43	40	13
1980	49	49	30
1983	51	50	33
1987	51	50	36

Source: Digest of Education Statistics 1987, table 150.

Percentage of degrees received by women in 1984 by field

	B.A.	M.A.	Ph.D.	Professional
Agriculture	32	28	15	
Architecture and environmental design	36	32	26	
Business and management	43	30	21	
Computer and information science	37	29	10	
Dentistry				20
Education	76	72	50	
Engineering	13	10	6	
Foreign Languages	73	68	55	
Health sciences	84	76	51	
Home economics	94	89	75	
Law	58	23	17	37
Letters	66	65	54	
Library and archival science	87	80	49	
Life sciences	47	45	31	
Mathematics	44	35	18	
Medicine				30
Military	8	1		
Pharmacy				53
Philosophy and religion	33	36	25	
Physical science	28	24	15	
Psychology	68	63	49	
Public affairs	68	62	45	
Social science	44	38	30	
Veterinary				47
Visual and performing arts	62	54	44	

Source: Digest of Education Statistics 1987, tables 152, 157.

Percentage of degrees received by minority women in 1981

	B.A.	M.A.	Ph.D.	Professional
American Indian/ Alaskan Native women	0.2	0.1	0.1	0.08
Asian or Pacific Islander women	0.9	0.9	0.7	0.7
Black women	4.0	4.0	2.0	2.0
Hispanic women	1.0	1.0	0.5	0.6

Source: Digest of Education Statistics 1987, tables 159, 160, 161, 162.

Percentage of women on university faculty

Year	Percentage
1869	12
1879	36
1889	20
1899	20
1909	20
1919	26
1929	27
1939	28
1949	25
1959	22
1969	24
1979	28
1981	27
1984	29

Source: Digest of Education Statistics 1987, table 100.

Women as a percentage of full-time instructional faculty in each rank in 1983

Full Professor	11
Associate Professor	22
Assistant Professor	35
Instructors	43
Lecturers	45

Source: *Digest of Education Statistics 1987,* table 138.

Percentage of minority women on faculty by rank in 1983

	Professor				
	Full	Assoc-ciate	Assis-tant	Instruc-tor	Lectur-er
American Indian/ Alaskan Native women	0.08	0.03	0.05	0.07 0.2	0.2
Asian or Pacific Islander women	0.7	0.3	0.5	1.0 0.8	1.5
Black women	1.9	0.6	1.3	2.5 3.4	3.3
Hispanic women	0.5	0.2	0.4	0.6 0.9	1.0

Source: *Digest of Education Statistics 1987,* table 138.

Selected
Bibliography

Books

Bernard, Jessie. *Academic Women.* Cleveland, Ohio: The World Publishing Company, 1964.

Center for Education Statistics, ed. *Digest of Education Statistics 1987.* Washington, D.C.: Center for Education Statistics, Office of Educational Research and Improvement, U.S. Department of Education, 1987.

Conable, Charlotte Williams. *Women at Cornell: The Myth of Equal Education.* Ithaca, N.Y.: Cornell University Press, 1977.

Dziech, Billie Wright, and Linda Wiener. *The Lecherous Professor: Sexual Harassment on Campus.* Boston: Beacon Press, 1984.

Farley, Jennie, ed. *Sex Discrimination in Higher Education: Strategies for Equality.* Ithaca, N.Y.: Cornell University Press, 1981.

Franklin, Phyllis, et al. *Sexual and Gender Harassment in the Academy: A Guide for Faculty, Students, and Administrators.* New York: Modern Language Association, 1981.

Furniss, W. Todd, and Patricia Albjerg Graham, eds. *Women in Higher Education.* Washington, D.C.: American Council on Education, 1974.

Horowitz, Helen Lefkowitz. *Campus Life.* New York: Alfred A. Knopf, 1987.

Howe, Florence. *Myths of Coeducation.* Bloomington, Ind.: Indiana University Press, 1984.

Howe, Florence, Suzanne Howard, and Mary Jo Boehm Strauss, eds. *Everywoman's Guide to Colleges and Universities.* New York: The Feminist Press, 1982.

Komarovsky, Mirra. *Women in College: Shaping New Feminine Identities.* New York: Basic Books, 1985.

Lasser, Carol, ed. *Educating Men and Women Together: Coeducation in a Changing World.* Urbana and Chicago: University of Illinois Press, 1987.

McGuigan, Dorothy Gies. *A Dangerous Experiment: 100 Years of Women at The University of Michigan.* Ann Arbor, Mich.: Center for Continuing Education of Women, 1970.

Perun, Pamela. *The Undergraduate Woman: Issues in Educational Equity.* Lexington, Mass.: D.C. Heath and Company, 1982.

Rix, Sara E., ed. *The American Woman 1987–1988: A Report in Depth.* New York: W.W. Norton, 1987.

Rossi, Alice S., and Ann Calderwood, eds. *Academic Women on the Move.* New York: Russell Sage Foundation, 1973.

Solomon, Barbara Miller. *In the Company of Educated Women: A History of Women and Higher Education in America.* New Haven: Yale University Press, 1985.

Stacey, Judith, Susan Bereaud, and Joan Daniels, eds. *And Jill Came Tumbling After: Sexism in American Education.* New York: Dell Publishing Company, 1974.

Till, Frank. *Sexual Harassment: A Report on the Sexual Harassment of Students.* Washington, D.C.: National Advisory Council on Women's Educational Programs, 1980.

Pamphlets

The Project on the Status and Education of Women of The Association of American Colleges (1818 R Street, N.W., Washington, D.C. 20009) publishes a number of useful, informative pamphlets, including:

"The Classroom Climate: A Chilly One for Women?"
"Sexual Harassment: A Hidden Issue"
"In Case of Sexual Harassment: A Guide for Women Students"
"Writing a Letter to the Sexual Harassor: Another Way of Dealing with the Problem"
"Title VII Sexual Harassment Guidelines and Educational Employment"
"Sex Discrimination Against Students: Implications of Title IX of the Education Amendments of 1972"
"The Problem of Rape on Campus"
" 'Friends' Raping Friends: Could It Happen to You?"
"The Age Discrimination Act of 1975 and Women on Campus"
"Re-entry Women: Special Programs for Special Populations"
"Selected List of Federal Organizations That Address Women's Issues"
"Centers for Research on Women"
"Minority Women's organizations and Programs"

The Office for Civil Rights of the United States Department of Education (Washington, D.C. 20202) publishes pamphlets such as "Sexual Harassment: It's Not Academic" and provides listings of local branches of the Office for Civil Rights.

The United States Equal Employment Opportunity Commission (EEOC) (2401 E Street, N.W., Washington, D.C. 20507) publishes pamphlets that include:
"Filing a Charge"
"Men and Women: Equal Work, Equal Pay"
"Title VII Enforces Job Rights"

The Feminist Press at The City University of New York offers alternatives in education and in literature. Founded in 1970, this nonprofit, tax-exempt educational and publishing organization works to eliminate sexual stereotypes in books and schools and to provide literature with a broad vision of human potential. The publishing program includes reprints of important works by women, feminist biographies of women, and nonsexist children's books. Curricular materials, bibliographies, directories, and a quarterly journal provide information and support for students and teachers of women's studies. In-service projects help to transform teaching methods and curricula. Through publications and projects, The Feminist Press contributes to the rediscovery of the history of women and the emergence of a more humane society.

NEW AND FORTHCOMING BOOKS

Black Foremothers: Three Lives, 2nd ed., by Dorothy Sterling. Foreword by Margaret Walker. Introduction by Barbara Christian. $9.95 paper.

Families in Flux (formerly **Household and Kin**), by Amy Swerdlow, Renate Bridenthal, Joan Kelly, and Phyllis Vine. $9.95 paper.

Get Smart! A Women's Guide to Equality on Campus, by Montana Katz and Veronica Vieland. $29.95 cloth, $9.95 paper.

Islanders, a novel by Helen R. Hull. Afterword by Patricia McClelland Miller. $10.95 paper.

Library and Information Sources on Women: A Guide to Collections in the Greater New York Area, compiled by the Women's Resources Group of the Greater New York Metropolitan Area Chapter of the Association of College and Research Libraries and the Center for the Study of Women and Society of the Graduate School and University Center of The City University of New York. $12.95 paper.

Lone Voyagers: Academic Women in Coeducational Universities, 1869–1937, edited by Geraldine J. Clifford. $29.95 cloth, $12.95 paper.

My Mother Gets Married, a novel by Moa Martinson. Translated and introduced by Margaret S. Lacy. $8.95 paper.

Not So Quiet . . . : Stepdaughters of War, a novel by Helen Zenna Smith. Afterword by Jane Marcus. $9.95 paper.

Ruth Weisberg: Paintings, Drawings, Prints, 1968–1988, edited and curated by Marion E. Jackson. With an essay by Thalia Gouma-Peterson. $15.00 paper.

Sultana's Dream and Selections from The Secluded Ones, by Rokeya Sakhawat Hossain. Edited and translated by Roushan Jahan. Afterword by Hanna Papanek. $16.95 cloth, $6.95 paper.

We That Were Young, a novel by Irene Rathbone. Afterword by Jane Marcus. $10.95 paper.

Women Activists: Challenging the Abuse of Power, by Anne Witte Garland. Foreword by Ralph Nader. Introduction by Frances T. Farenthold. $29.95 cloth, $9.95 paper.

Women Composers: The Lost Tradition Found, by Diane P. Jezic. Foreword by Elizabeth Wood. $29.95 cloth, $12.95 paper.

For a free catalog, write to The Feminist Press at The City University of New York, 311 East 94 Street, New York, NY 10128. Send individual book orders to The Talman Company, Inc., 150 Fifth Avenue, New York, NY 10011. Please include $1.75 for postage and handling for the first book, $.75 for each additional.